Medical Investigation 101 Workbook

Teacher's Edition

Interactive Assignments to Reinforce and Challenge Your New Medical Knowledge

Aligned to *Medial Investigation 101: A Book to Inspire Your Interest in Medicine and How Doctors Think*

by

Dr. Russ Hill

Dr. Richard Griffith

Illustrations by Raella Hill

Written and Published by

Dr. Russ Hill

Laguna Beach, California

and

Dr. Richard Griffith

Guilford, Vermont

Artwork images by Raella Hill

Laguna Beach, California

Introduction –

The STEM excursion into medical science for middle or high school students offers the hope of capturing the enthusiasm of students who may not have gotten excited about the more quantitative sciences. We all happen to own a human body that we interact with constantly, so perhaps no student will find this topic boring. We have tried in our writing to avoid topics that approach taboo boundaries for education in a teenage student population, however we appreciate that occasionally you, as the teacher, will most certainly have to navigate tricky questions that will certainly arise. I wish we had a foolproof solution to offer you, but realistically, you have learned how to deal with this problem from your own teaching experience.

In this teacher's edition of Medical Investigation 101, we hope to give you some extra background to the lessons, some answers we think fit with the questions in the text, and some ideas to perhaps make the lessons more engrossing. You deserve a little deeper insight into the material we offer your students.

We consider the recruitment of students to healthcare professions as one aim of our textbook, but more importantly we want this introduction to foster an appreciation of what keeps our bodies healthy and strong, and to provide a foundation for self-educational capabilities for our youth, so they can distinguish authoritative information for decisions they will need to make throughout their lives. We, therefore, ask you to encourage your students to research information in books and on the Internet for themselves as they learn about medical science. Your experience can guide them in separating high quality information from opinion and fad. If we accomplish that task and nothing more, the student will have achieved a goal worthy of their time and effort.

You, the teacher, will determine the success of this medical science introduction. We hope we have given you ammunition, but your enthusiasm and your quest for the adventure of learning will represent the true determinant of the success of this learning module. Thank you, most sincerely, for leading your talents to this effort.

Part 1

Medical science offers ten zillion different careers, and exploring the diversity of focus and type of work right up front allows students to wade into this field of science gently, recognizing some areas that may spark their curiosity.

1.1A Types of Physicians – Just as patients present to physicians with all types of complaints, hundreds of specialties and sub-specialties of physicians provide a spectrum of diagnostic talent. Invite your students to talk about their own health care adventures as they start to put names to the different sorts of physicians they may have encountered.

Next you can go to the roles they have only seen on TV or read about, and finally, perhaps they can talk with them about roles they never knew existed. It might prove fun to assign each student a short oral report on a healthcare role about which you discover no students in your class have any knowledge. Hearing the name of various medical roles spoken aloud often helps make these new words stick in their minds.

1.1B Physician Referrals – No doctor knows everything known about his or her area of expertise. Referrals occur when a difficult case requires additional knowledge and experience from another physician better capable of handling the situation. Students should understand physicians also work as a team by utilizing specialists, even sub-specialists, to find answers to difficult medical investigations. We ask students to put themselves in that role by selecting physician specialists they feel would best handle their referrals in the presented case studies.

1.2A Medical Support Team – Doctors readily get the focus of attention of students learning about health sciences, but we want to make sure your students appreciate that it takes an entire team, not just physicians, to provide the skills and expertise to deal with human disease and injury. In talking about all of these jobs we introduce more new words and more understanding of broad scope of medical science.

1.2B Medical Support Team Referrals – Just as no single physician can hold all the information available for diagnostic purposes, no doctors have the time and expertise required to perform all the individual tests and treatments for every known condition presenting for care. For this reason the entire medical support team works together to find the cause and, hopefully, successful treatment for the multitude of conditions that arise. In this section student select the support team member they would utilize to assist in the diagnosis or treatment of the cases presented.

If you have the chance, you might want to ask your students if they can perceive a different way we might organize healthcare. Our current system has lots of issues and we will eventually talk in the text about mistakes that occur in our system. We hope the next generation of medical scientists will find novel ways to make our system more efficient with better outcomes and less mistakes.

Part 2

2.0 The Medical Diagnostic Process – The text tries to introduce the classic notion of getting to a diagnosis by collecting information from the patient's history and from an examination of the patient, forming a list of possible causes for symptoms, and then systematically eliminating possible causes to get to the correct, specific diagnosis. We want the student to understand the wisdom of that approach, but we also want to go further so they can appreciate that in reality, medical practice may not follow that procedure. Sometimes the patient requires urgent attention before that process can play out, and sometimes the healthcare provider short-circuits the process in a manner that does not benefit the patient. Dr. Lawrence (Larry) Weed invented the problem oriented medical record that uses the SOAP notes we discuss in the text. As you teach students the classic approach, you need to understand that Dr. Weed found that doctors commonly were not going through the complete process with their patients, the way they had been trained to do. He fussed with his medical colleagues because they appeared to stop taking a full history as soon as they guessed a diagnosis. Some students might enjoy seeing Dr. Weed's talk about this, a humorous but serious talk, available on a YouTube video recorded years ago at Duke University. Sometimes the best way to learn about the right way to do something involves learning about the consequences of doing things the wrong way. Dr. Weed's talk falls into that category.

Students can try out the process of taking a medical history by role-playing in your classroom. We all love to act, and it can prove great fun to act the part of a sick patient explaining a pretend illness to another student playing the role of a physician. If the class enjoys that process, image inviting the principal by for your students to ask questions about his or her pretend aches and pains. Every student will remember that class for the rest of their lives. Inviting a healthcare professional from the community to stop in with a stethoscope, ophthalmoscope, and blood pressure cuff can also enliven this section of your class.

2.1 Chief Complaint – Surprisingly our healthcare system commonly forgets the patient's main reason for coming to see the doctor or other practitioner. You students might enjoy learning that the practitioner has been trained to think about the worst possible cause of every symptom first, while the patient wants to attribute every symptom to the mildest possible cause. This difference in perspective may lead to a misunderstanding, as illustrated by the patient who goes to the doctor complaining of a headache. The doctor thinks immediately about how to make sure the patient does not have a life threatening condition, like a stroke or brain tumor. All the proper tests get done and no terrible cause shows up. The doctor feels delighted with a job well done, but the patient feels terrible because the headache still hurts. We want the student to recognize that the chief complaint recorded correctly has great importance for the patient.

2.2 Medical History – Healthcare professionals have a specific format by which they record the patient's story about their illness to get as much help as possible figuring out the problem. We do not expect students at this level to do this well, because they have no background in pathophysiology needed to make sense of the details of symptoms. Still they may profit from trying out this role, and along the way become better patients by being able to recall the details of how symptoms came, to report accurately when they get sick or injured.

2.3 Review of Systems – A review of systems simply provides the practitioner a way to avoid missing important information the patient may have forgotten to include. For students in this course, we really only want to make them aware that important symptoms can occur in areas of the body not directly connected to the chief complaint, so they understand why practitioners ask them questions that may appear bizarre.

2.4 Medical Exam – Long ago physicians only had their own senses available to help them find evidence to identify the cause of a patient's illness or injury. Today we have a variety of laboratory tests and imaging technologies, but the physical examination of the patient still remains productive. Physicians spend hundreds of hours learning how to see, hear, feel, smell, but not taste, as was once the case, their patient to figure out the cause of the symptoms. We want the student to recognize that it takes a great deal of experience to accurately identify the abnormal from the normal.

2.5 Differential Diagnosis – Isabel Healthcare has a wonderful website that allows students to imagine a set of symptoms and get back a huge list of conditions that could cause those symptoms. When they try this out, they will probably find the number of possible causes overwhelming, especially since they will find conditions they have never even heard about. We do not want them to feel overwhelmed, although perhaps we do want them to glimpse the challenge of finding the true diagnosis that makes careers in medical care constantly challenging.

2.6 Diagnosis – Finally we get to the objective that will allow the application of a proper treatment. As you think about your role as a teacher, it may prove useful for you to appreciate that health care providers appear to get the diagnosis wrong perhaps as often as 1 in 5. Studies have found that autopsy diagnoses commonly differ from the diagnosis prior to a hospital death about that often. That observation might help students in this course recognize that great challenges exist in healthcare to make it possible for all patients to get the right treatment every time, and they might play a role in making that happen. The system does well today, but we still need bright, dedicated people to make it work better in the years ahead.

2.7 SOAP Notes – Larry Weed wanted to fix a problem. He found that patients reported problems that their doctors forgot about because they got focused on a different issue. These notes attempted to list all the problems and work through them in a way that nothing got lost. We want the student to appreciate the power of this organized way of keeping records. The way Weed did this can serve as a model for working on lots of tasks we all have to do in life. You might ask your students how they could use this sort of approach to decide what sport to play in school or what college they might decide to attend.

Part 3 - Investigations

Investigation 3.1A: Breathing Difficulty – The physiology of the lung deals mainly with the physics of gases. Students who have learned about ideal gas laws can appreciate all the things happening in the lung. The partial pressures of the different primary gases (oxygen, carbon dioxide, nitrogen, water vapor) have to add up to the total barometric pressure all along the anatomy. Students who get interested in the lung might want to read about how the lung balances blood flow to the flow of air for each region of the lung. How the body adjusts to climbing a tall mountain requires a thorough understanding of gas laws to appreciate how breathing faster can reduce the carbon dioxide inside the lung to raise up the partial pressure of oxygen needed to meet the body's needs when the total barometric pressure has fallen because of altitude. These sorts of questions allow students to appreciate the importance of the study of physics in addition to biology and chemistry when deciding on a career in medicine.

Investigation 3.1B: Pulmonary Embolism – Students may not appreciate that our blood passes through two sets of capillaries on a single circuit through the body. One set lies inside our lungs and the other set lies in all the other living organs in our body. If we have any glob of material in our blood stream (an embolus) larger than the opening in a capillary, that glob will come to rest either inside an organ or inside the lung. If the glob forms inside an artery, the problem occurs inside an organ (skin, gut, liver, brain, etc.). If the glob forms inside a vein, the problem occurs in the lung. When they understand this anatomy, everything in this case becomes clear.

Investigation 3.2A: Abdominal Pain – In medical school, students commonly love the study of gastroenterology (GI). The physiology of digestion, and the pathophysiology related to symptoms, both have an orderly predictability when compared with many other organ systems. This case we intended to highlight this model of understanding even though we do not expect the student to fully appreciate all the physiology and pathophysiology involved.

Investigation 3.2B: Virus vs Bacteria – Infection certainly forms a basic area of medical science, and this section introduces that huge dimension of medical practice. We think it important, however, for students to appreciate the fact that all microorganisms do not automatically pose a threat to human beings. You might want to share with your students the fact that some primitive tribes have a tradition of treating wounds with cow dung. Dung has millions of microorganisms. That works because the harmless microorganisms vastly outnumber the ones that cause harm, and therefore the harmful ones get essentially crowded out to the benefit of the patient. Since we go about killing microorganisms in our hospitals, when patients do get an infection, the infecting microorganism most likely has a resistance to all the things we use to disinfect, so that infection becomes deadly. Moreover we know now that some microorganisms actually help us survive. Some experts say that the average adult human may contain as much as 6 pounds of microorganisms that do important jobs on our behalf. Biologists have found that viruses may contain genes that help plants tolerate draughts, and do other things that help the plant survive and grow. They view this relationship as the plant storing some of its tricks in a virus, instead of keeping them in its own genes. Perhaps this method of storing abilities lowers the effort the plant needs to maintain such skills. You might think of these helpful viruses on a plant as a library of available tricks to keep the plant healthy.

Investigation 3.3A: Rib Pain – This case illustrates the notion that physicians do not need to treat every condition immediately, especially if they have doubts about the true diagnosis. In medicine and in life, doing nothing can often represent the wise option when no harm seems imminent. We all usually feel a need to take action, and find it very difficult to step back and watch until the correct action becomes clear.

Investigation 3.3B: Shingles – The idea that a virus hangs around dormant inside our body for years and years seems disturbing, but the authors thought it reasonable to alert the reader that the truth often seems stranger than anything we might imagine. The fact that shingles now has a very effective prevention with the use of a vaccine makes it ideal for young students to spread this news to their more senior members of their family. Just one more public service this lesson plan has to offer.

Investigation 3.4A: Sore Throat – This case illustrates that physicians have created a great many criteria to help them decide when to use specific therapies. Removing tonsils falls into that category, and many young people have a familiarity with this procedure. Having their own stories to tell about surgery allows them to share their experiences and deal with their questions and feelings about this episode of healthcare. Many people get interested in careers in medicine as a consequence of needing medical attention themselves in their youth. Someone may ask how we get along without tonsils, just as patients often ask how they can get along without an appendix. Probably the answer lies in recognition that for humans our world changes much more rapidly than we evolve, so we end up with some features that we may not need very badly today. Do we still need a little toe? Why do we have that little flappy thing at the bottom of our ear?

Investigation 3.4B: Role of Blood – Blood appears a necessity for multicellular organisms like animals, because not all cells in that situation can physically connect independently with the outside world. The blood, then, becomes the FedEx of the body, bringing in raw materials and removing waste from the cells. It also becomes the carrier of chemical communications (regulatory hormones and many medications) and the interstate to bring in special cells that fight invaders and repair damage. An amazing fluid!

We hope that understanding what blood can accomplish will make this red fluid less alarming for our students, and give them a new appreciation of how their body works. Do make sure that your students appreciate that red blood cells do not make the blood clot, that role falls to the platelets and a long list of proteins that reside in the plasma.

Investigation 3.5A: Emergencies – In our youth, we commonly lack patience. If we get students interested in healthcare, they predictably will want to do something about that interest now. This section on emergencies provides just that opportunity, since it alerts the reader to the possibility that in many communities they can take a course to learn to respond to emergencies. It would prove ideal to tell your students if these opportunities do exist in your community, and even invite a representative of the sponsoring organization to stop by the classroom.

3.5B: Chest Pain – This section on chest pain starts the process of understanding that a common, potentially serious symptom (chest pain) has many possible causes. You can ask the students to talk about how they would put together a strategy to respond when they cannot be sure if a particular patient has dangerous chest pain or perhaps something of little consequence going on. This discussion provides a great opportunity to talk about the need for planning for things to go wrong as a general characteristic of an individual's maturity. You can pick almost any human activity and ask students what might go wrong, and how they should plan for that possibility. You might surprise them by noting that bicycle riding, dog walking, and the use of bungee cords all create far more injuries that most of us recognize. People have head injury from flying off a bicycle, broken arms and legs when a dog decides to pull away suddenly, eye injuries from the recoil of a bungee cord. You can even add that users of powered snow blowers may wisely turn off the motor before trying to clear a foreign object stuck in the rotor, but still receive severe hand injuries because they fail to appreciate the torque that has built up in the drive mechanism, torque that does not go away when they turn off the motor. Hospitals see terrible hand injuries too frequently after a winter snowstorm.

Investigation 3.6A: Chronic Disease – When we cannot cure a disease or injury, we may have methods to reduce its ill effects so that people can carry on with their lives. This section helps students to appreciate the huge scope of medical practice devoted to managing conditions that never go away. As a society we invest money in research to try to make chronic conditions go away (cures). You might ask students to list chronic conditions they have seen, and then ask if they can think of any such conditions that research has eliminated. They probably should notice that we have many organizations devoted to helping people who suffer chronic diseases, perhaps because chronic conditions seem very unfair.

Investigation 3.6B: Diabetes – The section on diabetes simply takes the student a little deeper into a specific example of a chronic disease that seems quite unfair, has a society that raises money help to victims, has lots of ways to reduce the symptoms, and has active research to find a cure, most notably an artificial pancreas (thought to happen soon).

Investigation 3.7A: Shoulder Pain – Following on from chronic conditions, we take a closer look at joint problems that can prove chronic or quite acute. This look at orthopedics must certainly allow students to recognize that these physicians spend their time dealing much more with mechanical problems than the biology and chemistry that dominates in many other fields of health care. Healthcare needs people with very different interests and talents, or alternatively we can say that almost everyone can find an area of medical care that would fit their interests and abilities.

Investigation 3.7B: Joints – Our remarks immediately above apply to this section as well. We mention sports surgery on injured joints. Recently reports have emerged that "Tommy John surgery" done to repair the elbows of baseball pitchers now allows pitchers to throw faster after surgery than they could throw prior to their operation. As a result, reportedly some young pitchers with normal elbows are considering having the surgery. Students might enjoy talking about the notion that we could potentially use medical care to improve on normal, and would they think that appropriate, ethical, or wise?

Investigation 3.8A: Cough & Fever – This section gets into the nitty-gritty of office primary care so the student can picture himself or herself in that role, seeing patients with common symptoms and trying to figure out who needs special attention and who needs standard treatments. This role seems the classic foundation of medical practice, and thus highly important and equally non-glamorous. In the United States we think of TB as something near extinct, but around the world the majority of people commonly come in contact with this old and complex disease.

Investigation 3.8B: Lungs – Thinking about TB leads us to thinking about our lungs and the amazing process that goes on inside this fascinating organ. We do not talk about an artificial lung, but cardiac surgeons commonly make use of a machine that does the gas exchange job of the lung to allow them to stop a patient's heart for a repair. Physicians have used the same type of machines to treat patients with lung problems as well. Learning about how these machines works may help some students visualize how their own lungs work. An understanding requires the appreciation of how a gas can pass through a solid that may have been a part of some other science course they have studied.

Investigation 3.9A: Back Pain/Dark Urine – Just for variety, in this section we turn the mystery away from the disease and ask the reader to figure out the specialty they are playing. They will have to think back to the chapter they did at the beginning to remember what sort of doctors would go to see a patient complaining of dark urine. Among physicians, some believe that urologists seen to be among the happiest and most relaxed of any. Why that might prove true seems unclear. Perhaps they have such a high rate of successfully benefiting their patients that they get great satisfaction from there work. Ironically, we present here a case in which they do not have the ability to cure that patient. Your students may find it interesting that few students go to medical school to become urologists, but while in medical school they discover that this specialty offers them an opportunity to help people and have a highly rewarding career.

Investigation 3.9B: Urinary Tract – As we discuss the physiology of the urinary tract, the reader will probably not find urology compelling, which adds credence to the idea that the rewards of the practice of urology do not arise from the intellectual challenges of the specialty. We would argue that the kidney does an amazing task separating out the good from the bad in its quest to keep the blood stream pure and effective. Enough said.

Investigation 3.10A: Weak & Dizzy – Now we get more complex and become investigators. The authors borrowed this case from a real case from their experience in an effort to blend together some medical science with intrigue and some decision making in the social aspects of a case. This blend of tasks keeps medical practice a daily varying challenge and thereby pulls in bright young people interested in constantly testing their ingenuity.

Investigation 3.10B: Toxins – We live in a world contaminated with a variety of organisms and chemicals potentially harmful to our health. Illnesses caused by organisms have afflicted humanity for eternity. The industrial revolution that lifted mankind from the dark ages to its current state brought chemical toxins that impact our health. This chapter attempts to bring awareness of potential health risks inherent in our environment, habits, and lifestyle.

Investigation 3.11A: Foodborne Illness – This investigation represents a very common process in healthcare and gives the reader another experience of thinking through the diagnostic process. But this time we have background information up front and then get to the patient second. This case presents an opportunity to stress the importance of proper food handling, a too often under-utilized practice both in the home and commercially, as attested to by the approximately 48 million Americans encountering food poisoning each year.

Investigation 3.11B: Case Study – The reader by now should be pretty good at extracting a history of a disease from a patient, and can probably find fault with our set of questions. We want to take the mystery out of this process and make the student aware that they can do this and enjoy the process of sorting out the facts and getting to a solution. It serves as a reminder that leaving perishable foods unrefrigerated for prolonged periods increases their risk of foodborne illness.

Investigation 3.12A Head Injury – Now the exciting begins. All of medicine does not hinge on a thoughtful diagnostic process. Depending on the specialty, many or few instances of stark terror arise when decisions must be made quickly with limited information and action must take place to save a life. Here we have such a case. Hold on tight. We feared this case might distress our youngest readers, but apparently we misjudged the sophistication of the current generation; they seemed to love the fast pace of this case.

Investigation 3.12B Eye – The case we presented dealt with the brain, but the eye provided the key symptom, so we took that as an opportunity to discuss some of the unique marvels of the human eye. This section could fill volumes, but we kept to the essentials. The medicine of the eye comes primarily from physics, and the ophthalmologist office has a zillion dollars-worth of instruments to measure all of that physics. They usually do not depend so heavily on the patient's history. The eye truly represents a part of the brain that protrudes outside the skull, and you might want to share that perspective with your students. The analysis of what we see actually starts inside the eye, where it does image compression similar to the process used in high definition television. The optic nerve, therefore, differs from other nerves because it really consists of the neurons of the brain. Having said that, this section of the book mainly tries to present the fundamentals of how the eye does its job.

Investigation 3.13A: Brain – This section of the book we wrote several times. We began with an anatomical introduction to the brain in some detail, however, putting names on various parts of the brain does nothing a really explain how our brain works. How the brain works we can probably still classify as significantly unknown, but scientists know more and more every week. So as we rewrote this section we cut down the anatomy and wrote more about neural networks. The reader is not likely to finish this section with a great understanding of neural networks, but we hope with a good first step in an understanding of how we learn. We talk about backpropagation because computer simulated neural networks have a method to adjust the weightings of inputs to simulated neurons based on the ability of the network to get the correct final outcome. The correct and incorrect outcomes of the neural network feed a mathematical process called backpropogation that adjusts individual weightings so the entire network improves its performance with each evaluation of a training set of inputs.

Neurons in our brains do not work precisely this way. Instead we believe that each time an individual neuron fires, a physiological process involving protein synthesis adjusts the cell's sensitivity to each of its thousands upon thousands of inputs. The weights can be positive (stimulation) or negative (inhibition). The notion of feeding correct (desirable) outcomes or incorrect (undesirable) outcomes back into the network to create learning (improvement) comes about by virtue of the axons going in all directions, instead of due to a specific computation. The neuron's decision to fire comes from summing the weighted sum of all of its inputs.

Perhaps we still have not made that crystal clear. We all seem to understand that computers work on 1's and 0's and the accuracy of "on" and "off" creates the virtue of high reliability. The fact that a neuron either fires (similar to on) or does not fire (similar to off) encourages us to think of our biological brain as working much like a computer. Do not make that leap.

The decision to fire or not to fire a neuron uses a less reliable recipe than we find in digital computers. And the process of training our neurons (human learning) has much greater variation than the analogous process of programming a digital computer. Perhaps the variation makes us human, and therefore creative, or perhaps the variation leads to the quality we call creativity, and we then define that as an essential quality of humanity.

These ideas, we may argue, fall far outside the dimensions of this book, although the authors felt it important to mention the concept of neural networks and backpropogation because this appears to guide the growth of our understanding of the brain that will keep emerging. As the teacher, your job will lie in making what we mentioned in passing clear to all the students. We wish you good fortune as you do that. Sorry we could not be of any help.

Investigation 3.13B: Normal or Abnormal? – That is the question, we suppose. This section attempts to make a point that we believe often gets left unsaid in the teaching of medical science. We want our readers to appreciate that when we measure a feature of the human body and declare that a measurement in a specific range we will call normal, a process must exist to control that feature that we have measured. Too often we learn normal values in medical education without insisting that we also learn what goes on to keep that variable normal. In other words, normal does not happen by accident.

The purpose of the section lies not in explaining how the human body keeps things normal or allows them to become abnormal. Instead, we simply want each reader to appreciate that such a process exists, and to fully understand human physiology one ideally should understand the process at work to keep such a feature normal. If we do not understand that process, we have a ripe candidate for research. That sort of research becomes the means to better treatment outcomes.

Investigation 3.14A: Final Case—Our final case does not contain any final answers, but simply represents our challenge to our readers to think about what lies ahead in medical science. If they do elect a career in healthcare, they will see and do things we do not currently know how to predict... but we sort of try anyway.

Investigation 3.14B: Circle of Life – The practice of medicine requires not only scientific knowledge, but compassion and empathy for others. The manner in which physicians related to their patients incorporates the dimension of medical science that we sometimes call "bedside manner." We all have finite life spans currently, and we all reach some bargain with what we know and what we believe. Medicine bumps into life and death issues, and this section pays tribute to that dimension.

Investigation 3.15 – Looking Deeper - 5 Whys – We all depend upon the students who will decide to expend their life's time, energy, and talents to improve healthcare. We end the book with a plea that students continue to search for why, and the why behind each new answer to each question asked. Young children appear to do recursive questioning instinctively, but as we grow older we often seem to stop. Please ask your students not to stop!

Thank you, teacher, for inspiring your students to consider a career in healthcare. As our senior citizens continue to thrive with longer, more productive lives, the need for providers of health care rises. Projections by the Association of American Medical Colleges indicate a significant shortage of physicians by the year 2030 (about the time they will complete medical school). The U.S. Department of Labor projects major shortages of healthcare-trained personnel increasing each year until 2024. Your students' awareness of healthcare's rating as the number one growth industry over the next decade, one that cannot be outsourced to another country, should provide comfort and confidence of their ability to find a productive and meaningful career.

Table of Contents

Workbook Introduction 1

Introduction to Medical Investigation 2

Investigation 1.1 6

Investigation 1.2 17

Investigation 2.0/2.1 26

Investigation 2.2 31

Investigation 2.3/2.4 36

Investigation 2.5/2.6 45

Investigation 2.7 50

Investigation 3.1A 57

Investigation 3.1B 62

Investigation 3.2A 67

Investigation 3.2B 75

Investigation 3.3A 86

Investigation 3.3B 95

Investigation 3.4A 100

Investigation 3.4B 106

Investigation 3.5A 114

Investigation 3.5B 122

Investigation 3.6A 130

Investigation 3.6B 139

Investigation 3.7A 148

Investigation 3.7B 154

Investigation 3.8A 160

Investigation 3.8B 169

Investigation 3.9A 176

Investigation 3.9B 184

Investigation 3.10A 191

Investigation 3.11A 203

Investigation 3.11B 208

Investigation 3.12A 214

Investigation 3.12B 223

Investigation 3.12B 226

Investigation 3.13A 232

Investigation 3.13B 244

Investigation 3.14A/B 250

Investigation 3.15 257

Post-Script 260

About the Authors 262

Certificate of Achievement 264

Welcome to the *Medical Investigation 101 Workbook*. This workbook aligns with and supplements the material from *Medical Investigation 101*. It provides opportunities to reinforce and measure your learning from each chapter. The more medical terminology you master, and the more you understand about medical investigation, the better your preparation for future encounters with healthcare providers. Understanding how to transfer techniques for solving medical investigations to your analysis of decisions you make in your everyday life will serve you well. Understanding treatment modalities on the horizon can help you ask better questions and make better decisions when treatment options are discussed with your own physician. Should you find yourself pondering healthcare career choices, realizing the myriad of options may provide some light at the end of that tunnel.

The workbook includes assignments for each chapter and includes vocabulary research, reinforcing word match, and crossword puzzle. Assignments related to chapter content help galvanize important information and concepts. Extending activities provide an opportunity to think deeper and outside the box.

We encourage teachers to utilize the materials to foster improved medical terminology vocabulary and understanding of the healthcare system in all students. Whether students already demonstrate interest in healthcare careers, or simply care about how to communicate effectively with their physicians, everyone should find something of value in the material.

Thank you for choosing to enhance your *Medical Investigation 101* by utilizing this workbook. We hope you find it useful.

Assignment 1: **Vocabulary**

Directions: Use the text, a dictionary, or the internet to write a definition for each term.

1. physician: __**medical doctor or practitioner**__

2. pediatrician: __**physician who cares for children**__

3. specialist: __**doctor who treats only specific illnesses or parts of the body**__

4. diagnosis: __**the cause of the problem**__

5. treatment: __**a session of medical care using a drug or physical action**__

6. art of medical practice: __**dealing with patients in a caring and forgiving manner**__

7. science of medical practice: __**scientific knowledge of chemistry, physics, anatomy,**__ __**physiology & pathophysiology**__

8. physiology: __**details about how the human body normally works**__

9. pathophysiology: __**how illness or injury makes the body work abnormally**__

10. pathologist: __**specialist who often examines tissue under a microscope**__

11. history: __**the patient's story about how their health has changed**__

12. symptoms: __**a feeling or bodily feature that suggests illness or injury**__

13. abnormal: __**the opposite of normal**__

14. fracture: __**a break in a bone**__

Assignment 2: Vocabulary Match

Directions: Write the letter of the definition at the right next to the medical term on the left in the space provided.

1.   __K__   physician

2.   __D__   pediatrician

3.   __I__   specialist

4.   __G__   diagnosis

5.   __M__   treatment

6.   __B__   art of medical practice

7.   __N__   science of medical practice

8.   __E__   physiology

9.   __H__   pathophysiology

10.   __A__   pathologist

11.   __L__   history

12.   __C__   symptoms

13.   __J__   abnormal

14.   __F__   fracture

a.   A specialist who often examines tissue under a microscope

b.   Dealing with patients in a caring and forgiving manner

c.   A feeling or bodily feature that suggests illness or injury

d.   Physician who cares for children

e.   Details about how the human body normally works

f.   A break in a bone

g.   The cause of the problem

h.   How illness or injury makes the body work abnormally

i.   Doctor who treats only specific illnesses or parts of the body

j.   The opposite of normal

k.   Medical doctor or practitioner

l.   The patient's story about how their health has changed

m.   A session of medical care using a drug or physical action

n.   Scientific knowledge of chemistry, physics, anatomy, physiology & pathophysiology

Introduction

Vocabulary Assignment 3: Sentences

Dr._____

P.____ Date:_____

Directions: Use each word in a complete sentence.

1. physician: _____

   _____

2. pediatrician:_____

   _____

3. specialist: _____

   _____

4. diagnosis: _____

   _____

5. treatment: _____

   _____

6. art of medical practice: _____

   _____

7. science of medical practice: _____

   _____

8. physiology: _____

   _____

9. pathophysiology: _____

   _____

10. pathologist: _____

   _____

11. history: _____

   _____

12. symptoms: _____

   _____

13. abnormal: _____

14. fracture: _____

Medical Investigation

Directions: Use the highlighted terms in the chapter to solve the puzzle. Most clues come from the chapter text, but some require outside investigation. Omit spaces or dashes between words.

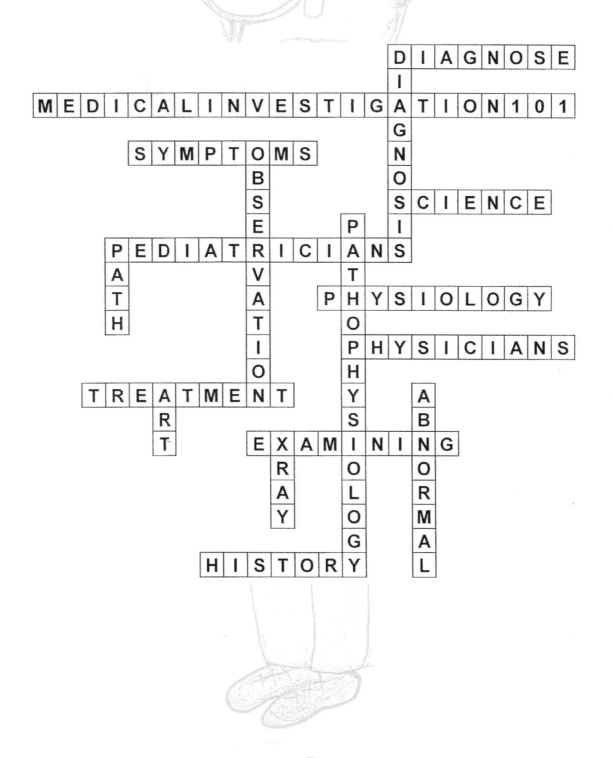

Types of Medical Doctors

Vocabulary Assignment 1A: Definitions

Directions: Use the text, a dictionary, or the internet to define these terms:

1. cardiologist: __a physician treating only heart problems__

2. sub-specialty: __an Orthopedic Surgeon who treats only knee problems__

3. catheter: __small tube inserted into a vein and threaded to the heart__

4. invasive cardiology: __Cardiologists who thread small tubes through veins into the heart__

5. gerontologist: __a physician treating only elderly patients__

6. tipping point: __The point at which small changes bring about a totally new solution__

7. artificial intelligence: __Programming computers to mimic the thought processes of humans__

8. hybrid thinking: __Blending computer processing with human skills to solve problems__

9. lifelong learning: __Type of learning required of physicians__

10. residency program: __training to become a specialist__

11. fellowship: __training to become a sub-specialist__

12. cardiothoracic surgeon: __treats severe injuries to the chest requiring surgery__

Investigation 1.1

Types of Medical Doctors

Vocabulary Assignment 1B: Definitions

Directions: Use the text, a dictionary, or the internet to define these terms:

1. neurosurgeon: __surgeon who operates on brain and spinal__

2. orthopedic surgeon: __treats bone and joint problems__

3. emergency physician: __triages patients with acute illness__

4. pediatrician: __treats only children__

5. oncologist: __treats cancer__

6. hematologist: __treats disorders of the blood__

7. nephrologist: __treats disorders of kidneys and urinary tract__

8. otolaryngologist: __treats problems to ears, nose, & throat__

9. dermatologist: __treats skin problems__

10. anesthesiologist: __puts patients to sleep so they don't feel pain during surgery__

11. toxicologist: __studies chemical exposure__

12. podiatrist: __treats problems of the feet and ankles__

Types of Medical Doctors

Vocabulary Assignment 2: Matching #1

Directions: Write the letter of the definition at the right next to the medical term on the left in the space provided.

1.   __K__   cardiologist

2.   __D__   sub-specialty

3.   __G__   catheter

4.   __A__   invasive cardiologists

5.   __H__   gerontologist

6.   __J__   tipping point

7.   __C__   artificial intelligence

8.   __I__   hybrid thinking

9.   __F__   lifelong learning

10.   __L__   residency program

11.   __B__   fellowship

12.   __E__   cardiothoracic surgeon

a. Cardiologists who thread small tubes through veins into the heart

b. Training to become a sub-specialist

c. Programming computers to mimic the thought processes of humans

d. Example: an Orthopedic Surgeon who treats only knee problems

e. Treats severe injuries to the chest requiring surgery

f. Type of learning required of physicians

g. Small tube inserted into a vein and threaded to the heart

h. Physician treating only the elderly

i. Blending computer processing with human skills to solve problems

j. The point at which small changes bring about a totally new solution

k. Physician treating only heart related problems

l. Training to become a specialist

Types of Medical Doctors

Vocabulary Assignment 2: Matching #2

Directions: Write the letter of the definition at the right next to the medical term on the left in the space provided.

1. __F__ emergency physician

2. __K__ pediatrician

3. __C__ oncologist

4. __N__ pathologist

5. __E__ nephrologist

6. __M__ otolaryngologist

7. __I__ dermatologist

8. __A__ anesthesiologist

9. __D__ toxicologist

10. __L__ podiatrist

11. __G__ plastic surgeon

12. __J__ pulmonologist

13. __B__ neonatologist

14. __H__ psychiatrist

a. Provides surgery pain-free

b. Treats only newborns

c. Treats cancer

d. Studies chemical exposure

e. Treats kidney diseases

f. Triages patients with acute illness or injury

g. Expert in cosmetic surgery

h. Treats only mental illness

i. Treats skin lesions

j. Treats respiratory tract problems

k. Treats only children

l. Treats only foot & ankle injuries

m. Treats ears, nose & throat

n. Examines tissue under microscope & performs chemical tests to diagnose disease

Investigation 1.1

Dr._____

Types of Medical Doctors

P._____Date:_____

Vocabulary Assignment 3B-1: Sentences

Directions: Write a complete sentence using each vocabulary term below.

1. specialties: _____

_____

2. sub-specialties: _____

_____

3. catheter: _____

_____

4. invasive cardiology: _____

_____

5. primary care: _____

_____

6. tipping point: _____

_____

7. artificial intelligence: _____

_____

8. hybrid thinking: _____

_____

9. lifelong learning: _____

_____

10. residency program: _____

_____

11. fellowship: _____

_____

12. cardiothoracic surgeon: _____

_____

Investigation 1.1

Dr._____

Types of Medical Doctors

P._____Date:_____

Vocabulary Assignment 3B-2: Sentences

Directions: Write a complete sentence using each vocabulary term below.

1. neurosurgeon: _____
   _____

2. orthopedic surgeon: _____
   _____

3. emergency physician: _____
   _____

4. pediatrician: _____
   _____

5. oncologist: _____
   _____

6. hematologist: _____
   _____

7. nephrologist: _____
   _____

8. otolaryngologist: _____
   _____

9. dermatologist: _____
   _____

10. anesthesiologist: _____
    _____

11. toxicologist: _____
    _____

12. podiatrist: _____
    _____

11

Medical Specialties Worksheet

Directions: Identify on the right side of the chart the area of expertise for each specialist on the left.

Physician Specialty	What types of problems or patients do they treat?
Gerontologist	the elderly
Oncologist	cancer
Dermatologist	skin lesions
Otolaryngologist	ear, nose, & throat
Internist	adults
Psychiatrist	mental problems
Orthopedist	bones & joints
Anesthesiologist	painless surgery
Pediatrician	children
Hematologist	blood disorders
Obstetrician	delivers babies
Cardiologist	heart problems
Neurologist	brain & nerve problems
Pathologist	examines tissue under microscope
Toxicologist	toxic chemical exposure
Infectious Diseases	communicable diseases
Gastroenterologist	stomach, intestine, & colon problems
Plastic Surgeon	skin & cosmetic problems
Neonatologist	newborns
Podiatrist	foot & ankle
Ophthalmologist	eye exams & surgery
Acupuncturist	relieves pain using needles & meridians
Dentist	tooth & gum disease
Pulmonologist	lungs & respiratory tract
Family Practice	adults & children; refers complex problems

Types of Physicians: Referrals

Since human minds find the human body quite complex, a single doctor cannot possibly treat every type of medical problem. Physicians routinely call on other doctors to help them when they feel that doctor can do a better job of solving the problem for the patient. When this happens it is called **referring** the patient.

In this activity **YOU** are the Family Practitioner. When patients come to you with problems you can easily solve, you take care of the patient yourself. But when you cannot confidently make a diagnosis on your patient's complaints you would <u>refer</u> that patient to another physician who has more experience with that type of problem.

What does it mean to "refer" the patient?

<u>To refer a patient is to send them to another physician specializing in or having more experience with that particular problem than you.</u>

In each situation below, to which physician would you most likely refer the patient?

1. A 45 year old male patient complains of ringing in their ears which has been present on and off for two months. You find no obvious reason for this, so you decide to refer the patient to a specialist. To which specialist would you probably send this patient?

    Patient 1: __**Otolaryngologist**_____

2. An 87 year old female is brought to you by her daughter because she goes for walks and get lost in her own neighborhood. She likes to drive her car but has trouble remembering where she parked it. The elderly lady constantly asks you the same question over and over. To which specialist would you probably refer this patient?

    Patient 2: __**Gerontologist**_____

3. The mother of a thirteen year old boy brings him into your office. She tells you her son fell off his skateboard while doing ramp jumping in the back yard. She believes he injured his left arm. You look at the arm and find the arm has swollen and the boy reports it feels very tender to the touch. You order an x-ray, which shows a break in the radius bone of the lower arm.
    a. Which bone do we call the radius? LARGER or **SMALLER** bone of the forearm

    b. Where would you refer this patient for further evaluation and treatment?
        Patient 3:__**Orthopedist   or Emergency Physician**_____

4. A 57 year old man comes to you because he is concerned that he occasionally feels light headed and gets dizzy. He cannot tell you any particular activity that causes this to happen. When you listen to his heart you hear an irregular heart beat and an abnormal sloshing sound between the normal beats of the heart.

   To which physician specialist might you consider referring this patient?

   Patient 4: ___**Cardiologist**___

5. A 21 year old female comes to your office complaining she always feels weak and tired. She says she sometimes sees black spots in her field of vision and occasionally experiences difficulty keeping her balance. You take a blood sample and look at it under the microscope. You find an abnormally low number of red blood cells.
   a. What important substance do red blood cells carry?

      ___**Oxygen**___

   b. To which specialist would you probably refer this patient?

      Patient 5: ___**Hematologist**___

6. A 35 year old female comes to you complaining of pain and numbness starting in her right hip and shooting down her right leg. Lifting heavy objects makes the pain worse and the pain has been growing progressively worse over the past several months. On examination you find the patient cannot feel sharpness on the skin of the right leg when touched with a sharp probe and cannot feel the difference between a warm and cold wet gauze when applied to the right leg.

   To which physician would you refer this patient?
   Patient 6: ___**Neurologist**___

7. A Mother brings in a nine year old girl after her pet cat scratched the girl's face. The mother is concerned the child might catch cat scratch fever. When you examine the wound you see a deep cut on the right cheek below the eye that goes deep enough to require stitches. You write a prescription for an antibiotic to protect the child from cat scratch fever, but you decide to refer the girl to a specialist for her stitches because very small, careful stitches may prevent her from developing a noticeable scar on her face.

   Who would you refer this patient to for facial stitches?

   Patient 7: ___**Plastic Surgeon**___

Crossword: Medical Specialties

Directions: Use the highlighted terms in the chapter to solve the puzzle. Most clues come from the chapter text, but some require outside investigation. Omit spaces or dashes between words.

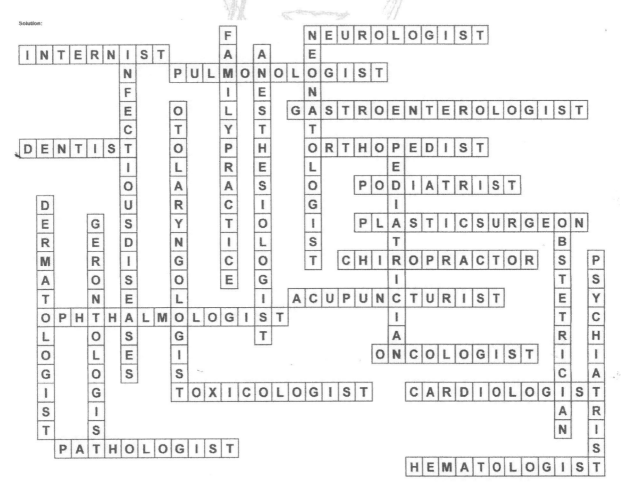

Solution:

Extension Activities:

1. Write a paragraph about what you think might be your greatest challenges to becoming a doctor.

2. Write a paragraph about your opinion of the greatest challenge for you in working as a doctor.

3. Write a paragraph about what you think would be the greatest reward to working as a physician.

4. If you were to become a doctor, what type of doctor would you want to be and why?

5. Write a five paragraph essay titled: Three Types of Doctor I Would Most Like to Be

6. Write a five paragraph essay titled: The Rewards of a Working as a Medical Doctor?

Medical Support Team

Vocabulary Assignment 1: Definitions

Directions: Use the text, a dictionary, or the internet to write a definition for each term below.

1. receptionist: _____ **greets patients and sets up appointments** _____

2. registered nurse: _____ **carries out treatment plans order by physicians & monitors patients' progress** _____

3. physician assistant: _____ **treats patients under the supervision of a physician, but is not a nurse** _____

4. nurse practitioner: _____ **a registered nurse (RN) with advanced training in diagnosing and treating illness** _____

5. physical therapist: _____ **helps patients reduce pain and improve or restore mobility** _____

6. optometrist: _____ **examines eyes and fits glasses and contact lenses and treats eye infections, but does not do eye surgery.** _____

7. speech therapist: _____ **helps those having speaking and language difficulties** _____

8. dental hygienist: _____ **cleans teeth, assesses for oral diseases, & provides preventive care under supervision of dentist** _____

9. pharmacist: _____ **specially qualified to prepare and dispense medicinal drugs** _____

10. occupational therapist: _____ **rehabilitates patients to perform daily and work related activities** _____

11. psychologist: _____ **studies mental processes and human behavior by observing, interpreting, and recording how people relate to one another** _____

12. chiropractor: _____ **performs diagnosis and manipulative treatment of misalignments of the spine** _____

Medical Support Team

Vocabulary Assignment 1: Definitions

Directions: Write the letter of the definition at the right next to the medical term on the left in the space provided.

1. __C__ receptionist

2. __K__ registered nurse

3. __G__ physician assistant

4. __I__ nurse practitioner

5. __B__ physical therapist

6. __J__ optometrist

7. __F__ speech therapist

8. __L__ dental hygienist

9. __A__ pharmacist

10. __H__ occupational therapist

11. __D__ psychologist

12. __E__ chiropractor

a. specially qualified to prepare and dispense medicinal drugs

b. helps patients reduce pain and improve or restore mobility

c. greets patients and sets up appointments

d. studies mental processes and human behavior by observing, interpreting, and recording how people relate to one another

e. performs diagnosis and manipulative treatment of misalignments of the spine

f. helps those having speech difficulties and language issues

g. treats patients under supervision of a physician, but not a nurse

h. rehabilitates patients to perform daily and work related activities

i. a registered nurse (RN) with advanced training in diagnosing and treating illness

j. examines eyes, prescribes glasses & contact lenses, treats infections

k. Carries out treatment plans order by physicians & monitors patients' progress

l. Cleans teeth, assesses for oral diseases, & provides preventive care under supervision of dentist

Investigation 1.2: Medical Support Team

Dr. _____

Vocabulary 3: Sentences

P._____ Date_____

Directions: Use each medical career below in a complete sentence.

1. receptionist: _____

_____

2. registered nurse:_____

_____

3. physician assistant: _____

_____

4. nurse practitioner: _____

_____

5. physical therapist: _____

_____

6. optometrist: _____

_____

7. speech therapist: _____

_____

8. dental hygienist: _____

_____

9. pharmacist: _____

_____

10. occupational therapist: _____

_____

11. psychologist: _____

_____

12. chiropractor:_____

_____

Medical Support Team Members

Medical Support Team Member   How they help Doctors & Patients

Pharmacist	Prepares & dispenses medicines
Dental Hygienist	Assesses oral disease & cleans teeth
Registered Nurse (RN)	Carries out physician treatment plan
Massage Therapist	Relaxes tight or painful muscles
Surgical Technician	Handles surgical instruments, assists surgeons
Phlebotomist	Takes & processes blood samples
Optometrist	Examines eyes, prescribes glasses & contacts, and treats eye infections
Orthopedic Technician	Assists orthopedist in surgery & office
Respiratory Therapist	Assesses & gives pulmonary treatments
Cardiology Technician	Performs tests assessing heart conditions
Medical Librarian	researches medical articles for physicians
Radiology Technician	Performs diagnostic tests using X-rays
Occupational Therapist	Rehabilitates patients to daily or work activities
Medical Records Clerk	Keeps patient charts current & complete
Nuclear Medicine Tech	Performs diagnostic tests using radioactive materials
Dental Assistant	Assists dentist, prepares filling & crowns
Speech Therapist	Assesses & treats speech difficulties
Chiropractor	Manipulative treatment of spine & soft tissue
Audiologist	Assesses hearing & dispenses hearing aids
Nurse Practitioner	RN with advanced training, treats & diagnoses
Clinical Psychologist	Studies mental processes & human behavior
Physical Therapist	Helps reduce pain & improve mobility
Ultrasound Technician	Performs radio wave tests on abdominal organs & pregnant women

1.2.5: Medical Support Team Referrals

Physicians diagnose the problem causing the patient's complaint and decide which treatments will help most. Since doctors often don't have the time or equipment necessary to administer the treatment themselves, they often refer the patient to a member of the Medical Support Team. For example, if you have a sore throat with a cough and green phlegm, the doctor might write a prescription for antibiotic pills. Most physicians do not keep all the medicines they prescribe in their office; instead they send you to a member of the support team that knows all about prescription medicines, called a Pharmacist.

Directions:

In this activity **YOU are the Family Practitioner**. When patients come to you with common problems where you know the answer but don't have what they need, you can refer them to the appropriate medical support team member. Your challenge here is to refer your patients to the appropriate support team member so they get the best results. **Select your answers from the support team members listed in Worksheet 1.2A and record your answers on the following pages.**

The Medical Support Team

Directions: Write the medical support team member who might best assist the patient and the physician in each situation.

Patient 1 is an 11 year old female who fell on her right wrist playing soccer. She felt immediate pain in the area and was brought to you for evaluation and treatment. An x-ray showed a small fracture, or break, in one of the bones of her wrist. She was placed in a cast for six weeks and the cast removed. Another x-ray showed the fracture healing well. The girl complained that her wrist was stiff and weak. You wrote her a prescription to visit which support team member?

Patient 1: ____**Physical Therapist**_____

Patient 2 is a 19 year old male who visits your office with a complaint of bad breath. You ask him if he has been to a dentist in the past year; his reply is : "No". When you look in his mouth you notice a small amount of redness (erythema) in his gums. You recommend a visit to a dentist as soon as possible. The Dentist examines his teeth and notes small pieces of rotten food between some of his teeth in addition to the erythema in his gum tissue. No cavities are found on the examination. Who would the Dentist refer this patient to for treatment?

Patient 2: ____**Dental Hygienist**_____

Patient 3 is a 63 year old female who visits your office with a complaint that her husband always accuses her of saying "What did you say?" "He thinks I can't hear him when he speaks; but I think he is just mumbling." You perform a simple hearing test and observe that her hearing appears to be affected in her left ear. You examine her for excess ear wax and find none. At this point you might consider referring this lady for further evaluation, but to whom?

Patient 3: _____**Audiologist**_____

Patient 4 is a 62 year old male who has been your patient for many years. About four months ago he suffered a stroke which left him with great difficulty speaking. You would like him to get help so that he can regain some of his speaking skills. Which medical support team member would you refer him to?

Patient 4: _____**Speech Therapist**_____

Patient 5 is a 73 year old male smoker who has been admitted to the hospital with difficulty breathing. Because he has smoked for over 50 years he has a previous diagnosis of emphysema. When you listen to the sounds coming from his lungs using your stethoscope you hear sounds consistent with pneumonia. Which medical support team member would you call on to help this patient breath more comfortably?

Patient 5: _____**Respiratory Therapist**_____

Patient 6 is a 51 year old male who visits you complaining of intermittent chest pain, which usually goes away when he stops walking or being active. Right now his chest does not hurt. Your testing machine is broken, so you refer him to the hospital to have an EKG test. Which member of the hospital support team would most likely perform this test on your patient?

Patient 6: _____**Cardiology Technician**_____

Patient 7 is a 39 year old female who has recently returned from a trip to Africa. She complains of intermittent fever and chills, and a lack of appetite. You want to know more about the current diseases occurring in Africa. Which member of the support team could help find the information so you can know the most likely diseases to consider?

Patient 7: _____**Medical Librarian**_____

Patient 8 is a 24 year old pregnant female wanting to attempt to determine the sex of her unborn baby. Which member of the support team could perform an ultrasound test that might provide that information?

Patient 8: _____**Ultrasound Technician**_____

Crossword 1.2.6: Medical Support Team

Directions: Use the highlighted terms in the chapter to solve the puzzle. Most clues come from the chapter text, but some require outside investigation. Omit spaces or dashes between words.

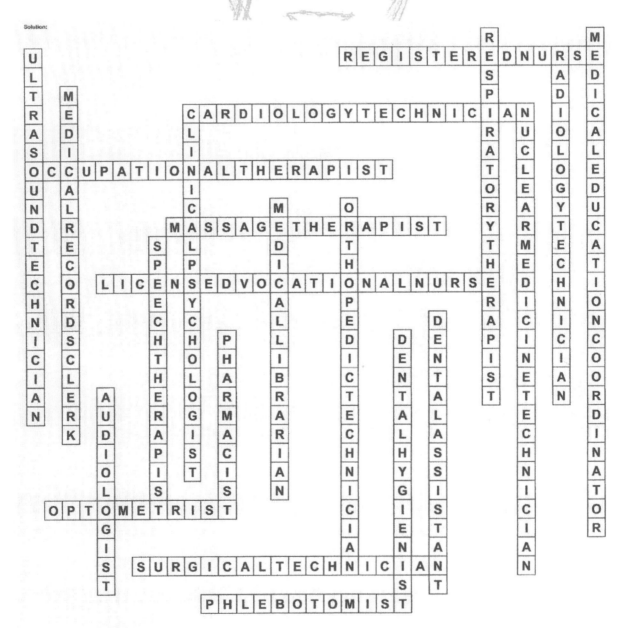

Extension Activities:

1. Write a paragraph about what you think might be your greatest challenges to becoming a healthcare support team member.

2. Write a paragraph about your opinion of the greatest challenge for you in working in a medical support team role.

3. Write a paragraph about what you think would be the greatest rewards to working as a medical support team member.

4. If you were to become a medical support team member, which role would you want to fill and why?

5. Write a five paragraph essay titled: Three Medical Support Members I Would Most Like to Be.

6. Write a five paragraph essay titled: The Rewards of a Career in Healthcare?

Medical Examination/Chief Complaint

Vocabulary 1: Definitions

Directions: Use the book or internet to write a definition for each medical term below.

1. subjective findings: __the information on the chart provided by the patient__

2. objective findings: __things an examiner observes during the examination, such as edema or erythema__

3. diagnosis: __the actual cause of the symptoms or change in health status__

4. scientific method: __a systematic approach consisting of hypotheses, observation, measurement, testing, and forming a conclusion__

5. art of medicine: __the creative skills the practitioner brings to the treatment of illness and injury__

6. chief complaint: __the patient's primary problem or complaint__

7. secondary complaints: __all other patient complaints after the main complaint or problem__

8. exacerbate: __to make the symptoms worse and more pronounced__

9. symptoms: __signs or changes in health status that could indicate illness or injury__

10. acute: __injury or condition having first occurred within the last few days or weeks__

11. chronic: __a condition of set of symptoms present for an extended period of time__

12. differential diagnosis: __the complete list of possible causes of the symptoms__

Medical Examination/Chief Complaint

Vocabulary 2: Matching

Directions: Write the letter of the definition at the right next to the medical term on the left in the space provided.

1. __B__ subjective findings

2. __G__ objective findings

3. __K__ diagnosis

4. __D__ scientific method

5. __I__ art of medicine

6. __A__ chief complaint

7. __E__ secondary complaints

8. __J__ exacerbate

9. __H__ symptoms

10. __F__ acute

11. __L__ chronic

12. __C__ differential diagnosis

a. the patient's primary problem or complaint

b. the information on the chart provided by the patient

c. the complete list of possible causes of the symptoms

d. a systematic approach consisting of hypotheses, observation, measurement, testing, and forming a conclusion

e. all other patient complaints after the main complaint or problem

f. an injury or condition having first occurred within the last few days or weeks

g. things an examiner observes during the examination, such as edema or erythema

h. signs or changes in health status that could indicate illness or injury

i. human creative skills the practitioner brings to the treatment of illness and injury

j. to make the symptoms worse and more pronounced

k. the actual cause of the symptoms or change in health status

l. a condition or set of symptoms present for an extended period of time

Investigation 2.0/2.1

Medical Examination/Chief Complaint

Vocabulary 3: Sentences

Dr. _____

P._____Date_____

Directions: Use each term below in a complete sentence.

1. subjective findings: _____

   _____

2. objective findings:_____

   _____

3. diagnosis: _____

   _____

4. scientific method: _____

   _____

5. art of medicine: _____

   _____

6. chief complaint: _____

   _____

7. secondary complaints: _____

   _____

8. exacerbate: _____

   _____

9. symptoms: _____

   _____

10. acute: _____

    _____

11. chronic: _____

    _____

12. differential diagnosis: _____

    _____

The Medical Diagnostic Process

1. How did medical practice probably begin thousands of years ago at the very beginning of man's evolution?

    People felt badly and by chance found that a certain food or activity allowed them to feel better. Likely they shared those experiences with others.

2. What does 'subjective' information refer to?

    Subjective refers the things told to you by the patient that you have not seen yourself, such as a headache or description of pain

3. How is 'objective' information different from 'subjective' information?

    Objective refers to things you can see yourself, such as measuring the amount of swelling or hearing abnormal heart sounds

4. What is a 'diagnosis'?

    The diagnosis is the cause of the symptoms or changes in your patient's health status

5. What does the word 'critical' mean when describing the condition of a patient?

    Critical refers to very serious illness, capable of causing death or major permanent disability

6. Describe the 'Scientific Method' as utilized in the practice of medicine.

    The Scientific Method as applied to the practice of medicine is a systematic approach of listening to the patient's history and complaints, considering all possible causes, performing and examination and tests, and eliminating all except the actual cause of the medical problem.

7. Describe how physicians use both **art** and **science** in treating patients.

    The art of medicine is how well you listen to and treat your patients, while the science of medicine utilizes what we know to find the cause and appropriate treatment of the problem.

Investigation 2.1

Dr._____

Activity 2.1

P.____Date:_____

Activity 2.1:

Think about the last time you went to the doctor. Did the nurse or doctor ask you questions like the ones above? Answer the questions above for that occasion (or make up a new problem) on a piece of paper. Now team up with a fellow student. Decide who will be the doctor and who will be the patient. The doctor will attempt to determine the patient's chief complaint details by asking questions. Then switch roles. Remember, medical investigation involves asking lots of questions. Ask each other these questions, and more if you think of additional questions related to their medical history or complaint.

- o   What makes it feel better?
- o   What makes you feel worse?
- o   Is the problem always in the same place or does it move around?
- o   What have you tried already before coming here?
- o   Is the problem constant or does it come and go?
- o   Is the problem getting better, worse, or staying the same?
- o   What activities **exacerbate** the problem?
- o   Does anyone else in your family have this problem?

Interview notes: (write down things you learn about your patient)

_____

_____

_____

_____

_____

_____

_____

_____

_____

_____

Medical History

Vocabulary 1: Definitions

Directions: Use the text, a dictionary, or the internet. Write a definition for each term below.

1. chief complaint: __the patient's primary problem__

2. medical history: __the past medical problems as related by the patient__

3. gender: __male or female__

4. lifestyle: __the habits that influence our lives__

5. genetic: __traits or diseases inherited from your parents__

6. medicines: __drugs prescribed to treat medical problems__

7. overdose: __taking too much of a medicine__

8. sub-acute: __an illness or injury that remains symptomatic after several weeks__

9. side effects: __unintended effects or symptoms caused by a treatment__

10. surgery: __an invasive procedure to locate or correct an anatomical problem__

11. art of medicine: __the part of medical practice that goes beyond the science__

12. judgement: __the ability to make the right decision__

Medical History

Vocabulary 2: Matching

Directions: Match the description on the right to the medical term on the left.

1. __B__ chief complaint

2. __H__ medical history

3. __E__ gender

4. __J__ lifestyle

5. __A__ genetic

6. __D__ medicines

7. __I__ overdose

8. __K__ sub-acute

9. __C__ side effects

10. __L__ surgery

11. __G__ art of medicine

12. __F__ judgement

a. traits or diseases inherited from your parents

b. the patient's primary problem

c. unintended effects or symptoms caused by a treatment

d. drugs prescribed to treat medical problems

e. male or female

f. the ability to make the right decision

g. the part of medical practice that goes beyond the science

h. the past medical problems as related by the patient

i. taking too much of a medicine

j. the habits that influence our lives

k. an illness or injury that remains symptomatic after several weeks

l. an invasive procedure to locate or correct an anatomical problem

Investigation 2.2

Medical History

Vocabulary 3: Sentences

Directions: Use each medical term below in a complete sentence.

1. chief complaint: _____
   _____

2. medical history: _____
   _____

3. gender: _____
   _____

4. lifestyle: _____
   _____

5. genetic: _____
   _____

6. medicines: _____
   _____

7. overdose: _____
   _____

8. sub-acute: _____
   _____

9. side effects: _____
   _____

10. surgery: _____
    _____

11. art of medicine: _____
    _____

12. judgement: _____
    _____

Activity 2.2.1: Noting important details in the medical history

It is important to make note of any positive medical history findings. Any positive findings in the medical history questionnaire should be confirmed with the patient. For example, "In the medical history you wrote that you have had diabetes for 5 years; is this correct?"

Using the information provided for Patients 1 and 2 on the following pages, circle boldly or highlight all positive factors in the patient's medical history. After you have identified all of the positives, role play with a partner. Take turns being the doctor. Interview your patient about the positives in their medical history. Ask questions about the positives to get more information.

Patient 1

Medical History

Patient Name: use your name or a pseudo-name of your choice

Age: 61 **Birthdate:** your birthdate   **Gender:**   Female

Occupation: outside sales

Chief Complaint: headaches and occasional palpitations in chest

Current Medicines: aspirin for headaches, Maalox for stomach upset, estrogen

Past Medical Conditions: stomach ulcer treated 10 years ago

Last medical Evaluation: 5 years ago

Childhood Illnesses: strep throat, pink eye, roseola

Past Medical History

1. Stomach ulcer treated 10 yrs ago
2. 2 children by C-section many years ago

Family Medical History

Mother: uterine cancer

Father: hypertension and heart condition

Siblings: older brother has heart condition and hypertension

Surgical History

Cataract left eye 2 years ago

C- Section 39 and 41 years ago

Hysterectomy age 54

Activity 2.2.1   **Patient 2**

Medical History

Patient Name: use your name or a pseudo-name of your choice

Age: 43 **Birthdate:** your birthday   **Gender:** Male

Occupation: jack hammer operator

Chief Complaint: numbness and tingling in fingers and hands, weakness in hands and arms

Current Medicines:

1. Aspirin 325 mg as needed for headaches and hand pain

2. Advair steroid inhaler

Past Medical Conditions:

1.   asthma since childhood

Last Medical Evaluation: 8 years ago

Childhood Illnesses:

1.   Chicken pox
2.   Measles
3.   Mumps

Past Medical History

1.   Asthma since childhood
2.   Allergies to cat dander, grasses and pollens
3.   Broken left wrist 11 years ago

Family Medical History

Mother: type 2 diabetes

Father: heart condition

Siblings: sister has type 1 diabetes

Surgical History

Tonsillectomy age 4

Appendectomy age 14

Wisdom teeth removed (4) age 23

Review of System/Exam

Vocabulary 1: Definitions

Directions: Use the text, a dictionary, or the internet to write a definition for each term.

1. review of systems: __part of the history taking where the physician asks the patient about each and every organ system to avoid missing any symptoms__

2. positives: __abnormal findings noted in the medical history or examination__

3. negatives: __information or symptoms not experienced by the patient or not found by the physician during the examination__

4. differential diagnosis: __the list of all possible causes of the symptoms under investigation__

5. chart: __the patient record of past and current medical information__

6. follow-up: __when the patient returns for re-evaluation of a problem__

7. contiguous: __the organs of an area of the body that touch one another__

8. auscultation: __listening to the sounds of the heart, lungs, and other organs, usually using a tethoscope__

9. paresthesia: __abnormal perception of tingling or prickling in peripheral nerves__

10. stethoscope: __the most often used medical instrument carried by most physicians about their neck__

11. tissue: __cells and their products making up the various materials in your body__

12. ultrasound: __the use of sound waves to visualize soft tissue structures__

Review of System/Exam

Vocabulary 2: Matching

Directions: Match the definitions at the right to the medical term at the left.

1. __E__ review of systems

2. __G__ positives

3. __K__ negatives

4. __C__ differential diagnosis

5. __H__ chart

6. __J__ follow-up

7. __D__ contiguous

8. __L__ auscultation

9. __A__ paresthesia

10. __I__ stethoscope

11. __B__ tissue

12. __F__ ultrasound

b. cells and their products making up the various materials in your body

c. the list of all possible causes of the symptoms under investigation

d. the organs of an area of the body that touch one another

e. part of the history taking where the physician asks the patient about each and every organ system to avoid missing any symptoms

f. the use of sound waves to visualize soft tissue structures

g. abnormal findings noted in the medical history or examination

h. the patient record of past and current medical information

i. the most often used medical instrument carried by most physicians about their neck

j. when the patient returns for re-evaluation of a problem

k. information or symptoms not experienced by the patient or not found by the physician during the examination

l. listening to the sounds of the heart, lungs, and other organs, usually using a stethoscope

a. abnormal perception of tingling or prickling in peripheral nerves

Investigation 2.3/2.4

Review of Systems/Exam

Dr. _____

P._____Date_____

Vocabulary 3: Sentences

Directions: Use each term below in a complete sentence.

1. review of systems: _____

_____

2. positives:_____

_____

3. negatives: _____

_____

4. differential diagnosis: _____

_____

5. chart: _____

_____

6. follow-up: _____

_____

7. contiguous: _____

_____

8. auscultation: _____

_____

9. paresthesia: _____

_____

10. stethoscope: _____

_____

11. tissue: _____

_____

12. ultrasound:_____

_____

Activity 2.3A: Charting Positives from the Medical History in Review of Systems (ROS)

Using the section titled **ROS** (doctors rarely write "Review of Systems"; doctors often abbreviate it ROS), use the sample medical history chart on the following pages to write in the positive past medical history (**Hx**) information you want available for review for patients one and two.

Patient 1: Medical History

Patient Name: use your name or a pseudo-name of your choice

Age: 43 **Birthdate:** your birthday   **Gender:** Male

Occupation: jack hammer operator

Chief Complaint: numbness and tingling in fingers and hands, weakness in hands and arms

Current Medicines:

1. aspirin 325 mg as needed for headaches and hand pain

2. Advair steroid inhaler

Past Medical Conditions:

  1.   asthma since childhood

Last Medical Evaluation: 8 years ago

Childhood Illnesses:

  1.   Chicken pox
  2.   Measles
  3.   Mumps

Past Medical History

  1.   Asthma since childhood
  2.   Allergies to cat dander, grasses and pollens
  3.   Broken left wrist 11 years ago

Family Medical History

Mother: type 2 diabetes, Alzheimers

Father: heart condition, prostate cancer

Siblings: sister has type 1 diabetes

Surgical History

Tonsillectomy age 4

Appendectomy age 14

Wisdom teeth removed (4) age 23

- **Use the space on the following page to make notes regarding your review of systems from patient #1. Write positive findings from history**

39

Investigation 2.3

Activity 2.3A

Patient 1

Dr._____

P._____Date:_____

Review of Systems

Patient Name: _____**Student's Name**_____ Age: ___**43**___ Gender: **M** F

ROS:

Mental Status: _____**headaches**_____

Cardiac (heart):

_____negative_____

Circulatory: _____negative_____

Respiratory(lungs):____**asthma and allergies to cat dander, grasses, & pollens**___

Digestive: _____negative_____

Urinary: _____negative_____

Reproductive: _____negative_____

Dermatologic: _____negative_____

Extremities: ____**numbness & tingling in fingers & hands, weakness in hands & arms**____

Areas of concern or requiring additional information:

Medications: Aspirin for headaches & hand pain, Advair inhaler for asthma

Occupation: Jack Hammer operator

Childhood Diseases: Chicken Pox

Fracture left wrist 11 yrs ago

Surgical: Tonsillectomy (age 4), Appendectomy (age 14), Wisdom teeth Extraction (age 23)

Family History: Mother: type 11 diabetes, Alzheimers. Father: heart condition, prostate cancer

Investigation 2.3

Activity 2.3B

Patient 2:

Medical History

Patient Name: use your name or a pseudo-name of your choice

Age: 61 **Birthdate:** your birthdate   **Gender:**   Female

Occupation: outside sales

Chief Complaint: headaches and occasional palpitations in chest

Current Medicines: aspirin for headaches, Maalox for stomach upset, estrogen

Past Medical Conditions: stomach ulcer treated 10 years ago

Last medical Evaluation: 5 years ago

Childhood Illnesses: strep throat, pink eye, roseola

Past Medical History

3. Stomach ulcer treated 10 yrs ago
4. 2 children by C-section many years ago

Family Medical History

Mother: uterine cancer

Father: hypertension and heart condition

Siblings: older brother has heart condition and hypertension

Surgical History

Cataract left eye 2 years ago

C- Section 39 and 41 years ago

Hysterectomy age 54

Investigation 2.3

Dr._____

Activity 2.3.B

P.____Date:_____

Patient 2

Review of Systems

Student selected information

Patient Name: _____**Student's Name**_____ Age: __**61**___ Gender: M **F**

ROS:

Mental Status: ____**headaches**_____

Cardiac (heart): ___**intermittent chest palpatations**_____

Circulatory: _____negative_____

Respiratory
(lungs):___**negative**_____

Digestive: _____**stomach ulcer (tx 10 yrs ago)**_____

Urinary: _____

Reproductive: _____**childbirth x 2, C-section**_____

Dermatologic: _____negative_____

Extremities: _____

Areas of concern or requiring additional information:

Last examination: 5 yrs ago_____

Headaches & Palpatations, Hx Stomach Ulcer_____

Currents medications: Maalox, estrogen_____

Surgical Hx: Cataract L eye 2 yrs ago, C-Section X 2, Hysterrectomy 7 yrs ago

Family Hx: Mother: Uterine CA, Father: hypertension & cardiac disease, Siblings: Brother has hypertension and cardiac disease_____

Investigation 2.4 – Medical Exam   Teacher

Activity 2.4: Body Systems

Directions: Match the body system that are part of your examination on the left with members of each system on the right.

1.   Cardiovascular System

2.   Digestive System, Primary

3.   Digestive System, Secondary

4.   Endocrine System

5.   Integumentary System

6.   Lymphatic System

7.   Muscular System

8.   Nervous System

9.   Reproductive System, Male

10. Reproductive System, Female

11. Respiratory System

12. Skeletal System

13. Urinary System

11 Nose, Pharynx, Larynx, Trachea, Bronchi, Lungs

8   Brain, Spinal cord, Nerves

13 Kidneys, Ureters, Urinary bladder, Urethra

4   Pituitary gland, Pineal gland, Hypothalamus, Thyroid gland, Parathyroid

3   Teeth, Salivary glands, Tongue, Liver, Gallbladder, Pancreas

6   Lymph nodes, Lymph vessels, Thymus, Spleen, Tonsils

1   Heart, Blood vessels

5   Skin, Hair, Nails, Sense receptors, Sweat gland, Oil glands

2   Mouth, Pharynx, Esophagus, Stomach, Small intestine, Large intestine, Rectum

10 Ovaries, Uterus, Fallopian Tubes, Mammary glands

12 Bones, Joints

7   Muscles

9   Testes, vas Deferens, Urethra, Prostate

Investigation 2.4

Activity 2.4

Activity 1: Testing the Plantar Response. Find a partner. Take off your shoes and socks. Have your partner sit on a table or desk with their feet hanging in a relaxed manner. Using a neurological hammer if you have one, or the eraser end of a pencil, rub the eraser along the outside surface of the bottom of your partner's feet, one foot, then the other foot. You should observe the big toe move downward without any effort from your partner.

When you get home you can check your brothers and sisters plantar reflexes by using the eraser end of a pencil. If you check your baby brother or sister you need to know that it is normal for very young children to have a positive test, or upward movement of the big toe. In older children and adults the big toe should move downward.

Teacher

Differential Diagnosis/Diagnosis

P._____Date_____

Vocabulary 1: Definitions

Directions: Use the text, a dictionary, or the internet to write a definition for each term.

a. differential diagnosis: __the list of possible causes of a set of symptoms__

b. priority: __your most important focus or interest__

c. rule out: __the process by which you remove an item from the differential diagnosis__

d. pulmonary: __related to the respiratory system__

e. cardiac: __pertaining to the heart__

f. musculoskeletal: __the body system consisting of bones, muscles, and joints__

g. diagnosis: __the cause of the symptoms investigated__

h. symptoms: __changes in health status that may provide clues about the cause__

i. infection: __what you get when invaded by pathogenic germs__

j. injury: __what you have when you sprain your ankle__

k. genetic disorder: __a disease passed on by parents to their children at birth__

l. communicable: __a disease capable of spreading to others__

45

Investigation 2.5/2.6

Teacher

Differential Diagnosis/Diagnosis

Vocabulary 2: Matching

Directions: Match the definitions at the right to the medical terms on the left.

1. __B__ differential diagnosis

2. __F__ priority

3. __K__ rule out

4. __D__ pulmonary

5. __I__ cardiac

6. __A__ musculoskeletal

7. __L__ diagnosis

8. __G__ symptoms

9. __E__ infection

10. __J__ injury

11. __H__ genetic disorder

12. __C__ communicable

a. the body system consisting of bones, muscles, and joints

b. the list of possible causes of a set of symptoms

c. a disease capable of spreading to others

d. related to the respiratory system

e. what you get when invaded by pathogenic germs

f. your most important focus or interest

g. changes in health status that may provide clues about the cause

h. a disease passed on by parents to their children at birth

i. pertaining to the heart

j. what you have when you sprain your ankle

k. the process by which you remove an item from the differential diagnosis

l. the cause of the symptoms investigated

Investigation 2.5/2.6

Dr. _____

Differential Diagnosis/Diagnosis

P._____ Date_____

Vocabulary 3: Sentences

Directions: Use each term below in a complete sentence.

1. differential diagnosis: _____

   _____

2. priority:_____

   _____

3. rule out: _____

   _____

4. pulmonary: _____

   _____

5. cardiac: _____

   _____

6. musculoskeletal: _____

   _____

7. diagnosis: _____

   _____

8. symptoms: _____

   _____

9. infection: _____

   _____

10. injury: _____

   _____

11. genetic disorder: _____

   _____

12. communicable: _____

   _____

Activity 2.5.4   **Differential Diagnosis for Headaches**

Headaches are another disorder having many potential causes. Suppose your patient complains of headaches and wants you to investigate what is causing them. You don't want to let your patient down. Make a Differential Diagnosis for headaches. Think of as many things that could cause a headache to occur. Then think about which are the most serious potential causes and place an 'S' (for serious) next to them. These would be the conditions or causes you would want to rule out first.   Ref: http://www.mayoclinic.org/symptoms/headache/basics/causes/sym-20050800

Headache Differential Diagnosis (DDx):

(Hint: According to the Mayo Clinic [2], there are seven primary causes of headaches and over twenty-five secondary causes of headaches) How many can you think of?

1. Cluster headache
2. Migraine (with and without aura)
3. Tension headache
4. Trigeminal autonomic cephalalgia (TAC)
5. Chronic daily headaches
6. Cough headaches
7. Exercise headaches
8. Alcohol, particularly red wine
9. Certain foods, such as processed meats that contain nitrates
10. Changes in sleep or lack of sleep
11. Poor posture
12. Skipped meals
13. Stress
14. Acute sinusitis - Arterial tears
15. Blood clot within the brain
16. Brain aneurysm
17. Brain tumor
18. Carbon monoxide poisoning
19. Chiari malformation Concussion
20. Dehydration
21. Dental problems
22. Ear infection (middle ear)
23. Encephalitis (brain inflammation)
24. Giant cell arteritis
25. Glaucoma
26. Hangovers
27. High blood pressure (hypertension)
28. Influenza (flu) and other febrile illnesses
29. Intracranial hematoma
30. Medications to treat other disorders
31. Meningitis
32. Monosodium glutamate (MSG)
33. Overuse of pain medication
34. Panic attacks and panic disorder
35. Post-concussion syndrome
36. Pressure from tight headgear, such as a helmet or goggles
37. Pseudotumor cerebri
38. Stroke
39. Toxoplasmosis
40. Trigeminal neuralgia
41. And there are more known causes

Diagnosis: Infection, Injury, or Genetic Cause

One of the initial challenges you have as a physician is to classify your patient's chief complaint. In this activity you will practice classifying disorders into their category.

Legend: Caused by Infection = **INF**   Caused by Injury = **INJ**   Genetic cause = **GEN**

1. ___**GEN**___ Natural Red Hair
2. ___**INJ**___ Sprained Ankle after soccer game
3. ___**INF**___ Stomach ache after eating potato salad at picnic
4. ___**INF**___ Pimples on face
5. ___**INJ**___ Concussion after football game
6. ___**GEN**___ Down Syndrome
7. ___**INF**___ Chicken Pox
8. ___**INF**___ Infected ingrown toenail
9. ___**GEN**___ Cystic Fibrosis
10. ___**GEN**___ Blue Eyes
11. ___**INJ**___ Fractured wrist after a fall
12. ___**GEN**___ Muscular Dystrophy
13. ___**INJ**___ Fractured Pelvis after a car accident
14. ___**INF**___ Polio
15. ___**GEN**___ Infant born with six toes on each foot
16. ___**INF**___ Ebola
17. ___**INJ**___ Quadriplegic after fall from roof
18. ___**INF**___ Small Pox
19. ___**INJ**___ 2nd degree burns after a fire
20. ___**INF**___ Tuberculosis   # Correct: _____ /20

SOAP Notes

Vocabulary 1: Definitions

Directions: Use the text, a dictionary, or the internet to write a definition for each term.

1. SOAP: _follow-up notes using Subjective, Objective, Assessment, Plan_

2. subjective: _how your patient has been feeling_

3. objective: _things you observe during your examination of a patient_

4. assessment: _your opinion or diagnosis as written in your soap notes_

5. plan: _tests you will perform to find the cause of your patient's symptoms_

6. edema: _a cause of soft tissue swelling_

7. extension: _straightening of a joint, such as your elbow_

8. flexion: _bending your knee_

9. prescription: _what you write to the pharmacist so your patient can get their medicine_

10. sickness: _what patients probably have when they visit their physician for a sore throat and cough_

11. injury: _an example is a deep cut on your arm resulting from a bike accident_

12. organization: _a key to success in school and a successful medical practice_

SOAP Notes

Vocabulary 2: Matching

Directions: Match the definitions at the right to the medical terms on the left.

1. __A__ SOAP

2. __J__ subjective findings

3. __H__ objective findings

4. __L__ assessment

5. __D__ diagnostic plan

6. __I__ edema

7. __B__ extension

8. __G__ flexion

9. __K__ prescription

10. __F__ sickness

11. __C__ injury

12. __E__ organization

a. follow-up notes using Subjective, Objective, Assessment, Plan

b. straightening of a joint, such as your elbow

c. an example is a deep cut on your arm resulting from a bike accident

d. tests you will perform to find the cause of your patient's symptoms

e. a key to success in school and a successful medical practice

f. what patients probably have when they visit their physician for a sore throat and cough

g. bending your knee

h. things you observe during your examination of a patient

i. a cause of soft tissue swelling

j. how your patient has been feeling

k. what you write to the pharmacist so your patient can get their medicine

l. your opinion or diagnosis as written in your soap notes

Investigation 2.7

Dr. _____

P. _____ Date _____

SOAP Notes

Vocabulary 3: Sentences

Directions: Use each term below in a complete sentence.

1. SOAP: _____

_____

2. subjective: _____

_____

3. objective: _____

_____

4. assessment: _____

_____

5. plan: _____

_____

6. edema: _____

_____

7. extension: _____

_____

8. flexion: _____

_____

9. prescription: _____

_____

10. sickness: _____

_____

11. injury: _____

_____

12. organization: _____

_____

Activity 2.7.4

SOAP Note Activity 1

1. What does the S in SOAP stand for? **Subjective, Objective, Assessment, Plan**

2. Write a definition of "Subjective Findings".

   Subjective findings are those told by the patient and not observed by the physician.

3. Give two examples of "Subjective Findings" from a hypothetical patient visit.

   a. **headaches, swollen ankles, stomach pain, numbness**

   b. **bloody nose yesterday, earache. Anything told by patient not observed by you.**

4. What does the 'O' in SOAP stand for? **Objective** findings

5. Write a definition of "Objective Findings"

   Objective findings are observable findings during the examination, such as erythema (redness), swelling (one ankle larger than other, etc)

6. Give two examples of "Objective Findings" from a hypothetical patient visit.

   a. **erythema (redness) of the skin, oozing pus from a wound**

   b. **yellowish discoloration of the eyes, open, bleeding wound on foot, anything else that is observed at the examination**

7. What does the A in SOAP stand for? **Assessment**

8. Write a definition of "Assessment" from your hypothetical patient visit notes.

   Your impressions on possible causes for the patient's problem.

9. Provide two examples of possible "Assessment" entries in your patient notes.

    a. **rule out cellulitis vs dermatitis**

    b. **rule out bladder infection vs nephritis**

    c. **any other situation where the possibilities are considered or diagnosis given**

10. What does the "P" in SOAP stand for? **The Treatment Plan**

11. Write a definition of "Plan" as it pertain to your patient notes.

    The plan details how you will move forward to solve the mystery, including tests to run or prescriptions for therapy or medications

12. Provide two examples of things you might write in your Plan for your hypothetical patient.

    a. **Rx CBC and UA (complete blood count and urinalysis), or Rx X-ray R Shoulder**

    b. **Rx Penicillin 500mg TID   or Any other plan for tests, consultation, or treatment**

13. What is the name of the physician who in 1968 first described the concept of "SOAP Notes"? **Dr. Weed**

14. What problem was Dr. Weed attempting to solve by the introduction of "SOAP Notes"?

    Dr. Weed presented a method to track patients' progress at subsequent visits so that physicians could quickly determine previous symptoms, tests, and findings, called problem oriented notes.

SOAP Note Activity 2

Directions: Make up a hypothetical patient of your own. Think of at least five entries for Subjective and Objective findings. You should have at least three entries in the Assessment and Plan sections. Write out a set of SOAP notes on that patient. (student input)

_____

_____

_____

_____

_____

_____

_____

_____

_____

_____

_____

_____

_____

_____

_____

_____

_____

_____

_____

_____

_____

Crossword 2.7.6   **Medical Diagnosis**

Directions: Use the highlighted terms in chapters 2.1 through 2.7 to solve the puzzle. Most clues come from the text, but some may require outside investigation. Omit spaces or dashes between words.

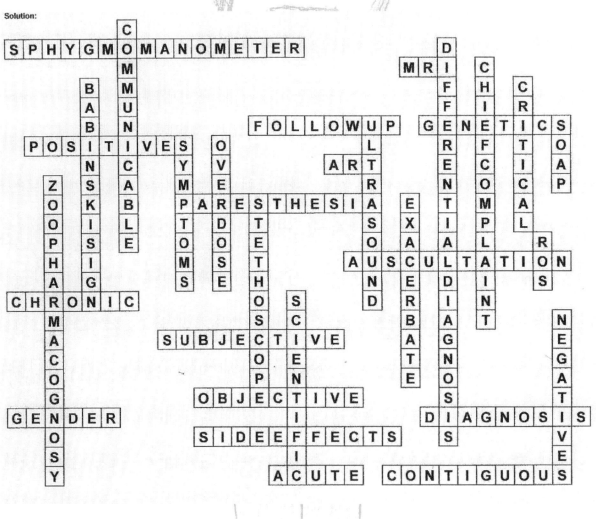

Breathing Difficulty

Vocabulary 1: Definitions

Directions: Use the text, a dictionary, or the internet to write a definition for each term.

1. agitated: _ **feeling or appearing troubled or nervous**

2. contract (as in "contract a disease"): **to become infected with an infectious disease**

3. sprain: **an injury characterized by stretching or rupture of one or more ligaments**

4. stethoscope: **primary physician tool for hearing heart, breath, and bowel sounds**

5. breath sounds: **sounds of air moving through lungs during inspiration and exhalation, and heard through a stethoscope**

6. oximeter: **instrument for measuring the proportion of oxygenated hemoglobin in blood**

7. oxygen saturation: **the percentage of oxygen-saturated hemoglobin compared to total blood hemoglobin**

8. pneumonia: _ **lung inflammation caused by bacterial or viral infection**

9. tuberculosis: **an infectious bacterial disease having growth of nodules in the lungs**

10. hiatal hernia: **protrusion of the stomach through the esophageal opening in the diaphragm**

11. pulmonary embolus: **a sudden blockage of an artery in the lung, usually caused by a clot moving from a leg vein**

12. obese: **severely overweight**

Investigation 3.1A

Breathing Difficulty

Vocabulary 2: Matching

Directions: Match each definition on the right to the medical term on the left.

1. __H__ agitated

2. __B__ contract

3. __J__ sprain

4. __A__ stethoscope

5. __L__ breath sounds

6. __E__ oximeter

7. __I__ oxygen saturation

8. __C__ pneumonia

9. __G__ tuberculosis

10. __F__ hiatal hernia

11. __K__ pulmonary embolus

12. __D__ obese

a. primary physician tool for hearing heart, breath, and bowel sounds

b. to become infected with an infectious disease

c. lung inflammation caused by bacterial or viral infection

d. severely overweight

e. instrument for measuring the proportion of oxygenated hemoglobin in blood

f. protrusion of the stomach through the esophageal opening in the diaphragm

g. an infectious bacterial disease having growth of nodules in the lungs

h. feeling or appearing nervous or troubled

i. the percentage of oxygen-saturated hemoglobin compared to total blood hemoglobin

j. an injury characterized by damage to one or more ligaments

k. a sudden blockage of an artery in the lung, usually caused by a clot moving from a leg vein

l. sounds of air moving through lungs during inspiration and exhalation, and heard through a stethoscope

Investigation 3.1A

Breathing Difficulty

Vocabulary 3: Sentences

Dr. _____

P._____Date_____

Directions: Use each term in a sentence.

1. agitated: _____

_____

2. contract:_____

_____

3. sprain: _____

_____

4. stethoscope: _____

_____

5. breath sounds: _____

_____

6. oximeter: _____

_____

7. oxygen saturation: _____

_____

8. pneumonia: _____

_____

9. tuberculosis:_____

_____

10. hiatal hernia:_____

_____

11. pulmonary embolus: _____

_____

12. obese: _____

_____

Investigation 3.1A

Breathing Difficulty

Worksheet 3.1.4

Breathing Difficulty Case 1 Worksheet

Directions: Answer the following questions based on Case 3.1: Breathing Difficulty.

1. What is the patient's Chief Complaint? __**Difficulty Breathing**__

2. What was the patient's Secondary Complaint? __accept **Sprained Ankle or Anxiety**__

3. How many breaths per minute were detected in the examination? __**<30**__/min

4. What is the normal rate of breathing for a patient her age: __**18**__/min

5. Using a watch with a second hand, count the number of breaths you take in a minute and record here: __**their own value**__ breaths/minute

6. What does an "oximeter" measure? __**blood oxygen saturation**__

7. What was the result of the oximeter test done on Betsy at the end of the examination?

   __**76**__%

8. What is the "normal" finding on the oximeter test? __**95 - 100**__%

9. What does Betsy's oximeter test result indicate?

   __**Betsy's blood carries an inadequate amount of oxygen**__

10. Do you think Betsy's ankle sprain could have caused Betsy's breathing difficulty?

    Circle: **Yes**　　　　No

11. Would you classify Betsy's condition as (circle one) **Acute** or Chronic

12. Would you classify Betsy's condition as (circle one):

    Possible Emergency or Probable Non-Emergency

13. From the chart below select the <u>top three</u> on your Differential Diagnosis List of things
    you want to <u>rule out</u> on this patient.

Differential Diagnosis	Yes	No
Pneumonia		X
Anxiety Reaction	**X**	
Pulmonary Embolus	**X**	
Asthma	**X**	
Pulmonary Hypertension		X
Heart Failure		X
Chronic Obstructive Pulmonary Disease		X
Tuberculosis		X

14. Do you think Betsy should be sent to a specialist for more evaluation or would you feel
    comfortable sending her home to rest for a few days before returning for further
    evaluation if the breathing difficulty continues?

    (Circle one)   **Send to Specialist**   or   Send Home to rest

15. If you sent Betsy to a specialist, to which one would you send her?

    Pulmonary Specialist (Pulmonologist)

Pulmonary Embolism

Vocabulary 1: Definitions

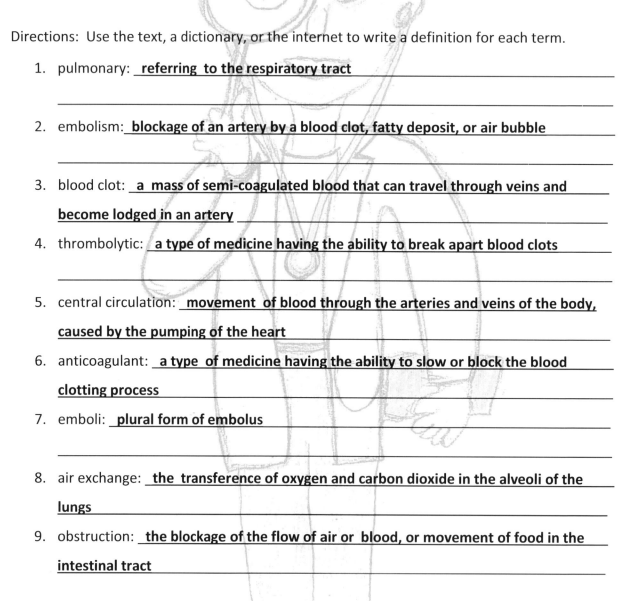

Directions: Use the text, a dictionary, or the internet to write a definition for each term.

1. pulmonary: __referring to the respiratory tract__

2. embolism: __blockage of an artery by a blood clot, fatty deposit, or air bubble__

3. blood clot: __a mass of semi-coagulated blood that can travel through veins and become lodged in an artery__

4. thrombolytic: __a type of medicine having the ability to break apart blood clots__

5. central circulation: __movement of blood through the arteries and veins of the body, caused by the pumping of the heart__

6. anticoagulant: __a type of medicine having the ability to slow or block the blood clotting process__

7. emboli: __plural form of embolus__

8. air exchange: __the transference of oxygen and carbon dioxide in the alveoli of the lungs__

9. obstruction: __the blockage of the flow of air or blood, or movement of food in the intestinal tract__

Pulmonary Embolism

Vocabulary 2: Matching

Directions: Match the definitions at the right to the medical terms on the left.

1. __D__ pulmonary

2. __H__ embolism

3. __A__ blood clot

4. __F__ thrombolytic

5. __B__ central circulation

6. __G__ anticoagulant

7. __I__ emboli

8. __C__ air exchange

9. __E__ obstruction

a. a mass of semi-coagulated blood that can travel through veins and become lodged in an artery

b. movement of blood through the arteries and veins of the body, caused by the pumping of the heart

c. The transference of oxygen and carbon dioxide in the alveoli of the lungs

d. Referring to the respiratory tract

e. a blockage of the flow of air or blood, or movement of food in the intestinal tract

f. a type of medicine having the ability to break apart blood clots

g. a type of medicine having the ability to slow or block the blood clotting process

h. blockage of an artery by a blood clot, fatty deposit, or air bubble

i. plural form of embolus

Investigation 3.1B

Pulmonary Embolism

Vocabulary 3: Sentences

Dr. _____

P._____Date_____

Directions: Write a sentence using each term.

1. pulmonary: _____

_____

2. embolism:_____

_____

3. blood clot: _____

_____

4. thrombolytic: _____

_____

5. central circulation: _____

_____

6. anticoagulant: _____

_____

7. emboli: _____

_____

8. air exchange: _____

_____

9. obstruction: _____

_____

Pulmonary Embolism

Directions: Answer the following questions.

1. What does the term "Pulmonary" refer to? **Pertaining to the lungs**

2. What is an "Embolism"? **Obstruction of an artery by a blood clot or air bubble**

3. What is an "Embolus"? **The blood clot, air bubble, or fat deposit that blocks a blood vessel**

4. Is a pulmonary embolism an acute or chronic problem? Explain your answer.

   A pulmonary embolism is an acute problem because it occurs suddenly. The patient suddenly has breathing difficulty because they cannot get enough oxygen. Depending on where the embolism occurs, death or sever disability can occur if the blockage is not corrected within minutes to hours.

5. What is the most likely cause of Betsy's pulmonary embolism?

   A blood clot probably travelled from the site of injury to her lung in a vein

6. Explain how a pulmonary embolism causes difficulty breathing?
   A pulmonary embolism causes difficulty breathing when it lodges in the bronchioles of the lung, blocking blood flood to the alveoli where air exchange occurs. Breathing becomes difficult when oxygen/carbon dioxide exchange is blocked. The patients breathes more rapidly and puts more strain on the heart.

7. What is a 'thrombolytic drug"? **A thrombolytic drug is a medicine designed to dissolve a blood clot and restore circulation to the afflicted area.**

8. Why is it important to begin thrombolytic drug therapy as soon as possible?
   The thrombolytic drug needs to be given as soon as possible to avoid as much tissue death as possible. Every minute of circulatory blockage increases the risk and amount of tissue death.

Investigation 3.1A/B

Teacher

Crossword 3.1.5A/B: **Pulmonary Embolism**

Directions: Use the highlighted terms in the chapter to solve the puzzle. Most clues come from the chapter text, but some require outside investigation. Omit spaces or dashes between words.

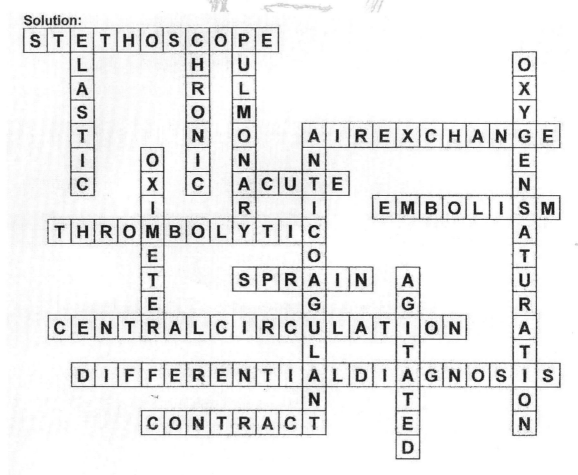

Solution:

Abdominal Pain

Vocabulary 1: Definitions

Directions: Use the text, a dictionary, or the internet to write a definition for each term.

1. abdominal cavity: __the space containing your lower esophagus, stomach, small intestine, colon, rectum, liver, gallbladder, pancreas, spleen, kidneys, and bladder__

2. quadrant: __division of the abdominal area into four areas placing the umbilicus in the center__

3. umbilicus: __your belly button or navel__

4. gurney: __a wheeled stretcher used to transport patients__

5. subtle: __very delicate or highly precise__

6. pancreatitis: __inflammation of the pancreas__

7. cholangitis: __a bacterial infection of the bile duct__

8. gastric: __referring to the stomach__

9. hepatoma: __cancer originating in the liver__

10. appendicitis: __inflammation and pain related to the appendix__

11. metastasis: __a secondary growth occurring away from the original site of cancer__

12. purulence: __synonym for pus__

Investigation 3.2A

Abdominal Pain

Vocabulary 2: Matching

Directions: Match each definition on the right with the medical term on the left.

1. __A__ abdominal cavity

2. __G__ quadrant

3. __J__ umbilicus

4. __C__ gurney

5. __K__ subtle

6. __L__ pancreatitis

7. __F__ cholangitis

8. __I__ gastric

9. __B__ hepatoma

10. __D__ appendicitis

11. __E__ metastasis

12. __H__ purulence

a. The space containing your lower esophagus, stomach, small intestine, colon, rectum, liver, gallbladder, pancreas, spleen, kidneys, and bladder

b. cancer originating in the liver

c. a wheeled stretcher used to transport patients

d. inflammation and pain related to the appendix

e. a secondary growth occurring away from the original site of cancer

f. a bacterial infection of the bile duct

g. division of the abdominal area into four areas placing the umbilicus in the center

h. synonym for pus

i. referring to the stomach

j. your navel or belly button

k. very delicate or highly precise

l. inflammation of the pancreas

Dr. _____

P._____Date_____

Directions: Write a sentence using each term.

1. abdominal cavity: _____

   _____

2. quadrant:_____

   _____

3. umbilicus: _____

   _____

4. gurney: _____

   _____

5. subtle: _____

   _____

6. pancreatitis: _____

   _____

7. cholangitis: _____

   _____

8. gastric: _____

   _____

9. hepatoma: _____

   _____

10. appendicitis: _____

   _____

11. metastasis: _____

   _____

12. purulence: _____

   _____

Abdominal Pain Worksheet

1. Name the four quadrants of the abdomen.

   a. **Upper right quadrant**

   b. **Lower right quadrant**

   c. **Upper left quadrant**

   d. **Lower left quadrant**

2. Which organs are located in the right upper quadrant?

   a. **Liver**

   b. **Right Kidney**

   c. **Gallbladder**

   d. **Colon**

   e. **Pancreas**

3. Which organs are found in the left upper quadrant?

   a. **Stomach**

   b. **Left Kidney**

   c. **Spleen**

   d. **Colon**

   e. **Pancreas**

4. What would you expect to find in the right lower quadrant?

   a. **Appendix**

   b. **Colon**

   c. **Small intestine**

   d. **Right Ureter**

   e. **Right Femoral Artery & Vein**

5. Which organs reside in the left lower quadrant?

    a. **Colon**

    b. **Small intestine**

    c. **Left Ureter**

    d. **Left Femoral Artery & Vein**

6. List the six clues given by Crystal's Mother in the history?

    a. **Very recent onset**

    b. **No friends had same symptoms**

    c. **Pain lower right quadrant of abdomen, radiating to right side**

    d. **Nausea & sweating**

    e. **Bloating**

    f. **Increased pain on moving**

7. Which six clues did you discover in your examination?

    a. **Temperature 101.9**

    b. **Pulse 92 bpm**

    c. **Respirations 22 / min**

    d. **Yellowish color to eye sclera**

    e. **Absent bowel sounds**

    f. **Rebound tenderness**

8. Which conditions did you eliminate from your initial differential diagnosis list?

    a. **peptic ulcer disease**

    b. **gastric cancer**

    c. **pancreatic cancer**

    d. **hepatoma**

    e. **abdominal aortic aneurysm**

    f. **chronic pancreatitis**

9. Which three conditions are the prime suspects in our investigation?

    a. Appendicitis

    b. Cholangitis

    c. Cholecystitis

10. Which three medical tests did you elect to order at the beginning of your investigation?

    a. CBC

    b. Urinalysis

    c. Abdominal Ultrasound

11. What was your final diagnosis?

    Appendicitis

12. What was your first treatment recommendation?

    Antibiotics

13. What treatment would you recommend if your initial treatment proved unsuccessful in curing Crystal's illness?

    Appendectomy (surgical removal of appendix)

14. Why was it important to treat this condition immediately and aggressively?

    If left untreated the appendix can rupture and cause peritonitis of the entire abdominal cavity, which can be fatal.

15. What are the primary risks inherent in any surgical procedure?

    a. Infection

    b. Excessive bleeding

16. Identify the structures in each abdominal quadrant shown below.

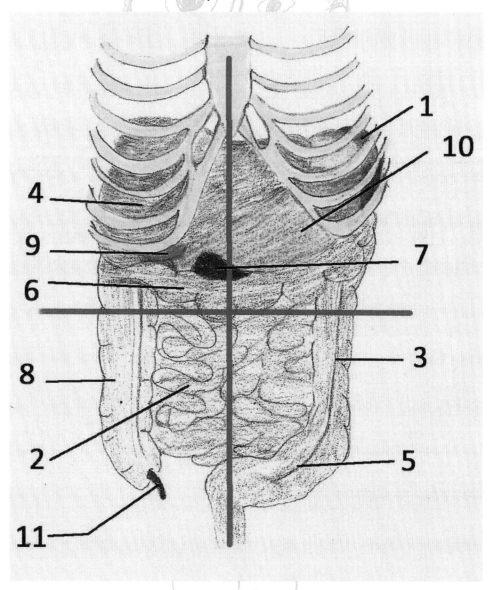

Directions: Write the name of the organ identified by each number in the diagram above.

1. **spleen**

2. **small intestine**

3. **descending colon**

4. **liver**

5. **Sigmoid colon**

6. **transverse colon**

7. **pancreas**

8. **ascending colon**

9. **gall bladder**

10. **stomach**

11. **appendix**

Crossword 3.2A   **Abdominal Pain**

Directions: Use the highlighted terms in the chapter to solve the puzzle. Most clues come from the chapter text, some require outside investigation. Omit spaces or dashes between words.

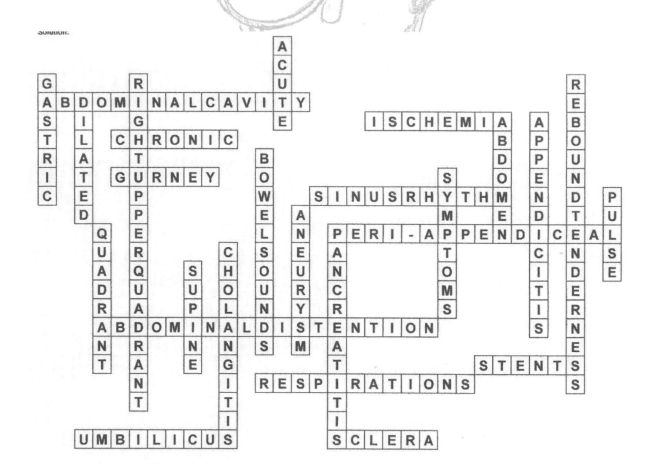

Solution:

Microbes 1

Vocabulary 1A: Definitions

Directions: Use the text, a dictionary, or the internet to write a definition for each term.

1. miasma: __highly unpleasant or unhealthy smelling air__

2. microorganisms: __organisms so small they can be seen only with a microscope__

3. carrier: __a person infected with an infectious disease agent , but who has no symptoms__

4. immunity: __an organism's ability to resist a disease or infection__

5. membrane: __a thin, flexible material that acts as a boundary or lining__

6. pores: __small openings through which gases, liquids, or microorganisms can pass__

7. virus: __a 'non-living' infectious organism capable of multiplying only in a hosts living cells and visible under an electron microscope__

8. rabies: __a fatal and contagious viral disease afflicting mammals and spread in saliva__

9. microbes: __a microorganism causing disease__

10. bacteria: __one-celled living organisms visible with a light microscope, some of which cause disease__

11. nanometer: __one-billionth of a meter__

12. antibiotic: __a medicine having the ability to kill or prevent reproduction of bacteria__

Investigation 3.2B   Teacher

Microbes 1

Vocabulary 2A: Matching #1

Directions: Match the definitions on the right to the medical terms on the left.

1. __C__ miasma

2. __E__ microorganisms

3. __B__ carrier

4. __D__ immunity

5. __J__ membrane

6. __G__ pores

7. __K__ virus

8. __I__ rabies

9. __H__ microbes

10. __L__ bacteria

11. __A__ nanometer

12. __F__ antibiotic

a. one-billionth of a meter

b. a person infected with an infectious disease agent , but who has no symptoms

c. highly unpleasant or unhealthy smelling air

d. an organism's ability to resist a disease or infection

e. organisms so small they can be seen only with a microscope

f. a medicine having the ability to kill or prevent reproduction of bacteria

g. small openings through which gases, liquids, or microorganisms can pass

h. a microorganism causing disease

i. a fatal and contagious viral disease afflicting mammals and spread in saliva

j. a thin, flexible material that acts as a boundary or lining

k. a 'non-living' infectious organism capable of multiplying only in a hosts living cells and visible under an electron microscope

l. one-celled living organisms visible with a light microscope, some of which cause disease

Investigation 3.2B

Dr. _____

Microbes 1

P._____Date_____

Vocabulary 3A: Sentences

Directions: Write a sentence using each term.

1. miasma: _____

_____

2. microorganisms:_____

_____

3. carrier: _____

_____

4. immunity: _____

_____

5. membrane: _____

_____

6. pores: _____

_____

7. virus: _____

_____

8. rabies: _____

_____

9. microbes: _____

_____

10. bacteria: _____

_____

11. nanometer: _____

_____

12. antibiotic: _____

_____

Microbes 2

Vocabulary 1B: Definitions #2

Directions: Use the text, a dictionary, or the internet to write a definition for each term.

1. super-infection: **a second infection occurring on top of or following an original infection**

2. communicable: **capable of being shared or spread to others**

3. vaccine: **stimulates the production of antibodies to prevent a disease**

4. febrile: **having an elevated body temperature**

5. pandemic: **a disease prevalent or spreading over an entire country or the world**

6. preventive: **measures taken to prevent the onset or spread of diseases**

7. epidemiologist: **a scientist who studies the spread and control of diseases**

8. unilateral: **visible or occurring on only the left or right side**

9. paralysis: **the inability to move a part or an entire body**

10. viable: **capable of surviving in a given environment**

11. syndrome: **a set of signs and symptoms that appear together and define a medical condition**

12. abscess: **a swollen, inflamed area of tissue containing an area of pus**

Microbes 2

Vocabulary 2B: Matching #2

Directions: Match the definitions on the right to the medical terms on the left.

1. __F__ super-infection

2. __D__ communicable

3. __L__ vaccine

4. __K__ febrile

5. __C__ pandemic

6. __J__ preventive

7. __G__ epidemiologist

8. __B__ unilateral

9. __E__ paralysis

10. __H__ viable

11. __A__ syndrome

12. __I__ abscess

a. a set of signs and symptoms that appear together and define a medical condition

b. visible or occurring on only the left or right side

c. a disease prevalent or spreading over an entire country or the world

d. capable of being shared or spread to others

e. the inability to move a part or an entire body

f. a second infection occurring on top of or following an original infection

g. a scientist who studies the spread and control of diseases

h. capable of surviving in a given environment

i. a swollen, inflamed area of tissue containing an area of pus

j. measures taken to prevent the onset or spread of diseases

k. having an elevated body temperature

l. stimulates the production of antibodies to prevent a disease

Investigation 3.2B

Microbes 2

Dr. _____

P._____Date_____

Vocabulary 3B: Sentences

Directions: Write a sentence using each term.

1. super-infection: _____

_____

2. communicable: _____

_____

3. vaccine: _____

_____

4. febrile: _____

_____

5. pandemic: _____

_____

6. preventive: _____

_____

7. epidemiologist: _____

_____

8. unilateral: _____

_____

9. paralysis: _____

_____

10. viable: _____

_____

11. syndrome: _____

_____

12. abscess: _____

_____

Worksheet 3.2B

Viruses & Bacteria Worksheet

Answer the following questions based on your reading of chapter 3.2B.

1. Name four ways bacterial and viruses differ.

     a. **Bacteria are living things; viruses are not**

     b. **Bacteria are larger than viruses**

     c. **Viruses do not contain mitochondria**

     d. **Bacteria treated with antibiotics; viruses prevented with vaccination**

2. Similarities between bacteria and viruses:

     a. **Microscopic size**

     b. **Symptoms of illness similar**

     c. **Similar methods of spreading**

     d. **Both cause millions of deaths each year**

3. Name four ways bacteria and viruses spread:

     a. **Water (contamination)**

     b. **Air (breathing)**

     c. **Insects (mosquitos, ticks)**

     d. **Direct human contact (touching contaminated objects)**

4. True or False: All bacteria are harmful to humans.

     False

5. Where do viruses reside?

     Inside living cells

Viruses & Bacteria

6. What do viruses require in order to survive?

    A living host

7. About what percent of bacteria cause infection?

    ~1%

8. What was the first antibiotic used to fight bacterial infection?

    Penicillin

9. Why is penicillin not very effective treating most infections today?

    Bacteria have adapted by developing resistance

10. What problem is caused by the overuse of antibiotics?

    Super-infections that do not respond to currently available antibiotics

11. What is the most effective method of preventing viral infection?

    Vaccination

12. What are four impossible measures that would almost guarantee that you would not

    catch a viral or bacterial infection?

    a. **Stop breathing**

    b. **Don't touch anything**

    c. **Don't eat food or drink water**

    d. **Don't go outside**

Worksheet 3.2B, page 3

Viruses & Bacteria

13. Name four serious viral infections spread by mosquitos.

   a. **Dengue fever**

   b. **Yellow Fever**

   c. **West Nile Fever**

   d. **Zika**

14. Which organism has probably killed more people than any other in the last 100 years?

   Flu virus

15. Which two insects transmit many of the most virulent viruses?

   a. **Mosquitos**

   b. **Ticks**

16. Which animals most commonly carry the rabies virus?

   a. **Skunks**

   b. **Raccoons**

   c. **Bats**

   d. **Foxes**

   e. **Coyotes**

17. What preventive treatments are given to those bitten or scratched by an animal suspected of possibly having rabies?

   a. **5 shots over 28 days**

   b. **rabies antibodies**

18. Why is it important NOT to breathe water into your nose when swimming in a public swimming pool or lake?

Sometimes single-celled organisms such as amoebas enter the body by way of the nose and work their way past the blood brain barrier and into the brain, where they are extremely difficult to treat. The result is often death of the patient

19. How does polio affect girls and boys differently?

   a. **Girls: scoliosis**

   b. **Boys: unilateral limb muscle wasting and paralysis**

Worksheet 3.2B, page 4

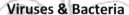

Viruses & Bacteria

20. Aside from organisms contaminating drinking water, what else can end up in water that can cause illness?

    Toxic chemicals such as lead

21. Name two bacteria that can cause food poisoning.

    c. **Salmonella**

    d. **E. Coli**

22. What are three bacteria that can infect humans when breathed in?

    e. **Staphylococcus**

    f. **Streptococcus**

    g. **Tuberculosis**

23. How long have bacterial and viruses existed on Earth?

    Billions of years

Crossword 3.2B   **Microbes**

Directions: Use the highlighted terms in the chapter to solve the puzzle. Most clues come from the chapter text, some require outside investigation. Omit spaces or dashes between words.

Solution:

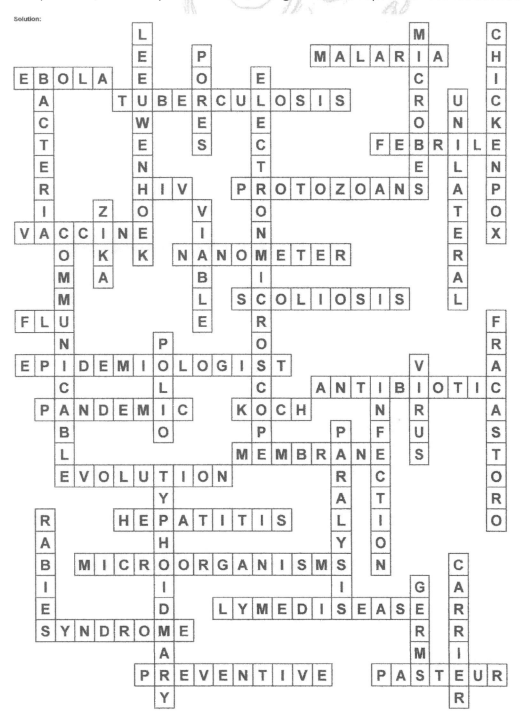

Rib Pain

Vocabulary 1: Definitions

Directions: Use the text, a dictionary, or the internet to write a definition for each term.

1. fracture: __a crack or break in a bone__

2. appetite: __your desire and need for food__

3. depression: __a persistent feeling of sadness and lack of interest__

4. fibromyalgia: __chronic musculoskeletal pain, fatigue, or tenderness on an area or areas__

5. brachial plexus: __the network of nerves sending signals to and from your spine and shoulder, arm, and hand__

6. stroke: __sudden death of brain cells due to arterial blockage or rupture__

7. multiple sclerosis: __a progressive degenerative neurological disease causing numbness, speech impairment, fatigue, & loss of coordination__

8. palpate: __to examine an area by touching__

9. elicit: __to induce a reaction to a stimulus__

10. thorax: __the area of the body between the neck and abdomen__

11. unilateral: __related to or affecting either right or left side, but not both sides__

12. bilateral: __relating to or affecting both left and right sides__

Rib Pain

Vocabulary 2: Matching

Directions: Match the definitions on the right to the terms on the left.

1. __C__ fracture

2. __G__ appetite

3. __A__ depression

4. __F__ fibromyalgia

5. __H__ brachial plexus

6. __L__ stroke

7. __K__ multiple sclerosis

8. __I__ palpate

9. __B__ elicit

10. __D__ thorax

11. __J__ unilateral

12. __E__ bilateral

a. a persistent feeling of sadness and lack of interest

b. to induce a reaction to a stimulus

c. a crack or break in a bone

d. the area of the body between the neck and abdomen

e. relating to or affecting both left and right sides

f. chronic musculoskeletal pain, fatigue, or tenderness on an area or areas

g. your desire and need for food

h. the network of nerves sending signals to and from your spine and shoulder, arm, and hand

i. to examine an area by touching

j. related to or affecting either right or left side, but not both sides

k. a progressive degenerative neurological disease causing numbness, speech impairment, fatigue, & loss of coordination

l. sudden death of brain cells due to arterial blockage or rupture

Investigation 3.3A

Rib Pain

Vocabulary 3: Sentences

Directions: Write a sentence using each term.

Dr: _____

P._____Date_____

1. fracture: _____
   _____

2. appetite:_____
   _____

3. depression:_____
   _____

4. fibromyalgia: _____
   _____

5. brachial plexus: _____
   _____

6. stroke: _____
   _____

7. multiple sclerosis: _____
   _____

8. palpate: _____
   _____

9. elicit: _____
   _____

10. thorax: _____
    _____

11. unilateral: _____
    _____

12. bilateral: _____
    _____

Patient Workup

1. **Chief Complaint: Burning pain ribs on right side**

2. **History of Chief Complaint:** (important points on present complaint)

    a. **burning pain right rib area 2 days duration**

    b. **can't sleep**

    c. **no appetite**

3. **Review of Systems:** (list known past or present medical conditions)

    a. **History of measles and chicken pox**

    b. **borderline type II diabetes**

    c. **No history of rib fracture, abdominal pain, or chest pain**

4. **Examination:**

    Wt = **178** lbs.   Respirations: **19** /min   Pulse: **88** /min
    Blood Pressure: **158 / 92**   Temperature = **98.5° F.**

    Heart: no abnormal sounds, regular sinus rhythm

    Lungs: clear

    Chest exam:

    a. **pain along right T-6 rib for a distance of 6 – 8 inches**

    b. **no bruising or discoloration**

    c. **no enlarged nodes**

    d. **no palpable mass**

    Why do you think the examination was limited to the chest area on this patient?

    This is a regular patient whom you have seen before presenting with a new complaint of rib area pain.

Worksheet 3.3A1.4 - Patient Workup

Page 2

5. **Differential Diagnosis:**

Disorder	Acute/ Chronic	Pain ↑ moving/ breathing	Swollen lymph nodes	Head aches	rash	Uni or bi-lateral	Stiff joints	Numb ness	blisters	Dia-rhea
Muscle strain	A	X				U				
Rib Fracture	A	X				U		X		
Fibromyalgia	C	X		X		U/B	X			X
Food poisoning	A		X	X						X
Lung Cancer	C	X	X							
Brachial plexus injury	A	X				U		X		
Shingles	A/C			X	X	U			X	X
Stroke	A/C					U		X		
Multiple sclerosis	C	X				U/B				

6. **Medical Tests:** Which, if any, of the <u>following</u> tests would you have considered if Ed had returned to the office in two days with no change in his condition?

Summary of Available Tests to Consider and what information they can provide your medical investigation:

Which test(s) would be most appropriate at this time? (check any that apply)

   X   **X-rays** of the chest and ribs

_____   **MRI** of the chest and ribs

_____   **Rib Biopsy**

_____   **CBC** blood test

_____   **Ultrasound** of chest and ribs

   X   **Prescription** for pain medication

Worksheet 3.3A1.4 - Patient Workup

Page 3

7. **Treatment Options:**

Which treatment would be most appropriate while waiting for test results:

_____ **Emergency Surgery** to remove the painful rib.

_____ **Radiation therapy** to kill any cancer that may be starting to grow in the rib.

__X__ **Prescription** for narcotic pain killer to allow patient to sleep for the next few nights until he returns for a progress check and more thorough examination.

_____ **Prescriptions for all antibiotics** that work on the four most common organisms causing infections.

__X__ **No Treatment** until all tests come back with results on the cause of the pain. (This is a reasonable alternative)

8. **Test Results**

   What were the X-ray results received from the radiologist?

   - **No fracture or dislocation;**
   - **Lungs clear**
   - **Pleural cavities clear**

9. **Diagnosis: What is your Diagnosis?**

   Acute Shingles episode

   What information led you to that diagnosis?

   Acute pain right rib area

   Returned in two days with blisters in T-6 dermatomal distribution

   History of chicken pox without shingles vaccination

   Patient age is > 60 years old

Worksheet 3.3A1.4 - Patient Workup

Page 4

10. Treatment Options:

Which treatment might you prescribe first? **pain medication**

Based on Ed's history and **symptoms** and your knowledge, is your step #1 treatment all that will be required? Yes   **No**

Are there other treatment **modalities** that might be helpful in making your patient comfortable? **Yes**   No

Select the treatment(s) below that would give your patient the best chance for relief in the **acute phase** of this disease

X if yes Blank if no	Treatment	purpose
X	Acetaminophen	Pain management
	Oral antibiotics	Stop bacterial infection
	Oral Anti-viral meds	Stop viral infection
	Oral Corticosteroids	Stop inflammatory response in body
	Antibiotic cream	Stop skin infection in blisters
X	Steroid cream	Stop inflammation of skin

Can shingles spread from one person to another? What about Shingles spreading Chicken Pox? If so, how? (You may have to read ahead in 3.3B to find the answers)

Method of spreading	yes	no
Through the air		X
Blister to skin contact with another person who has had chicken pox		X
Blister to skin contact with another person who has not had chicken pox	X	
Touching contaminated object		X
Sharing a glass		X
Contact with contaminated blood		X
Contact with contaminated urine		X
Cannot be spread to others		X

Worksheet 3.3A2.5 - Reflections

Reflections:

What was your patient's chief complaint? **Pain right rib area**

Would you consider Ed's complaint to be: (circle) **Acute** or Chronic

Why? **Symptoms started only two days ago**

_____

_____

How would you classify Ed's condition (circle your answer)?

      Possible Emergency   or   **Probably Non-Emergency**

Which DDx possibilities did you **rule out** right away?

 a. multiple sclerosis

b. lung cancer

c. stroke

Is Ed's condition an injury or **illness**? (Circle your answer)

If Ed's condition is an illness, is it **curable**? (circle answer)   Yes   **No**

Why or why not? **Once you have chicken pox you carry the virus causing Shingles in your body forever.**

_____

Was this injury or illness preventable? How or why not? **Preventable by having the vaccination for Shingles if over age 60.**

_____

_____

Crossword 3.3A   **Rib Pain**

Directions: Use the highlighted terms in the chapter to solve the puzzle. Most clues come from the chapter text, some require outside investigation. Omit spaces or dashes between words.

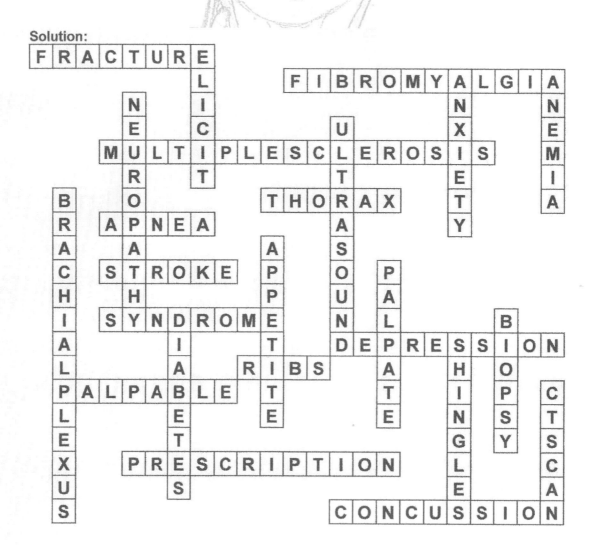

Solution:

Shingles

Vocabulary 1: Definitions

Directions: Use the text, a dictionary, or the internet to write a definition for each term.

1. shingles: **preventable illness that can occur in those having had chicken pox**

2. chicken pox: **childhood disease that can come back many years later as shingles**

3. dormant: **suspension or slowing of physical activities for a period of time**

4. blisters: **small fluid-filled bubble on the skin caused by friction or burn**

5. rash: **inflammation of the skin, often including redness and itching**

6. encephalitis: **inflammation of the brain caused by infection or allergic reaction**

7. vaccine: **drugs that create immunity to specific bacteria or virus infections**

8. neuralgia: **intense pain along the course of a nerve**

9. steroid: **medicines used to reduce swelling and inflammation, such as cortisone**

10. transplant: **organs that can be replaced from a donor**

11. immune system: **the system that protects the body from infection and disease**

12. preventable: **an illness that can be prevented with a vaccine**

Investigation 3.3B

Shingles

Vocabulary 2: Matching

Directions: Match the definition on the right to the medical term on the left.

a. medicines used to reduce swelling and inflammation, such as cortisone

1. __I__ shingles

b. suspension or slowing of physical activities for a period of time

2. __E__ chicken pox

3. __B__ dormant

c. inflammation of the skin, often including redness and itching

4. __G__ blisters

d. an illness that can be prevented with a vaccine

5. __C__ rash

e. childhood disease that can come back many years later as shingles

6. __F__ encephalitis

f. inflammation of the brain caused by infection or allergic reaction

7. __K__ vaccine

8. __L__ neuralgia

g. small fluid-filled bubble on the skin caused by friction or burn

9. __A__ steroid

h. organs that can be replaced from a donor

10. __H__ transplant

11. __J__ immune system

i. preventable illness that can occur in those having had chicken pox

12. __D__ preventable

j. the system that protects the body from infection and disease

k. drugs that create immunity to specific bacteria or virus infections

l. intense pain along the course of a nerve

Investigation 3.3B

Shingles

Vocabulary 3: Sentences

Directions: Write a sentence using each medical term in the space provided.

1. shingles: _____
   _____

2. chicken pox:_____
   _____

3. dormant: _____
   _____

4. blisters: _____
   _____

5. rash: _____
   _____

6. encephalitis: _____
   _____

7. vaccine: _____
   _____

8. neuralgia: _____
   _____

9. steroid: _____
   _____

10. transplant: _____
   _____

11. immune system: _____
   _____

12. preventable: _____
   _____

Shingles Worksheet 3.3B.4

Shingles

Directions: Answer the questions on your reading of Medical Investigation 3.3B.

1. Which virus causes chickenpox and shingles? **varicella-zoster virus**

2. How can you protect yourself from contracting chickenpox?
   Get vaccinated

3. How can your grandparents assure they do not contract Shingles?
   Get the shingles vaccination

4. What fraction of people over age 60 get Shingles?   **1/3**

5. How can the same virus that causes chickenpox in children and young adults cause shingles in grandparents? **The virus causing chicken pox stays in the body in a dormant state until it re-activates and causes shingles**

6. Describe the order of steps of Shingles presentation in a patient who previously had chickenpox?
   1. **The virus becomes active after laying dormant for years**
   2. **Pain, itching, & tingling on one side of the body or face**
   3. **A rash occurs within a few days**
   4. **Blister appear within a few more days**
   5. **Slight fever, headaches, chills, or an upset stomach may occur**
   6. **The blisters scab over in 7 to 10 days and go away in 2 to 4 weeks**
   7. **Pain can last much longer than the rash and blisters**

7. What are some of the rare complications that can occur in Shingles?

   blindness, hearing loss, pneumonia, or encephalitis, even death

8. How old are most victims of Shingles?   **most are over age 60**

9. What procedures can reduce the spread of the virus from Shingles blisters?

   Covering the rash and blisters

10. Which is more contagious, Shingles or **Chickenpox**? (circle your choice)

Investigation 3.3B Shingles   Teacher

Crossword 3.3B.5: Shingles

Directions: Use the highlighted terms in the chapter to solve the puzzle. Most clues come from the chapter text, but some require outside investigation. Omit spaces or dashes between words.

Solution:

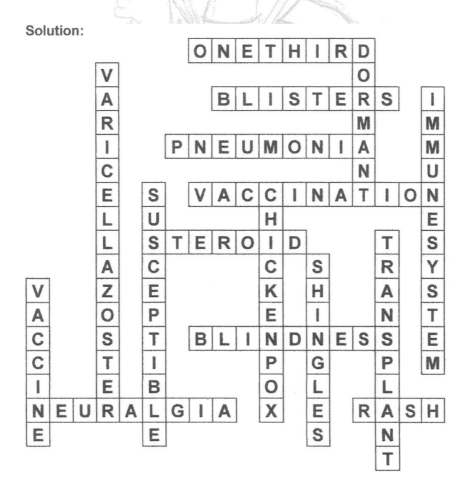

Sore Throat

Vocabulary 1: Definitions

Directions: Use the text, a dictionary, or the internet to write a definition for each term.

1. erythema: **redness of skin or tissue**

2. tympanic membrane: **thin tissue layer that separates external and middle ear; vibrates to transmit sound waves**

3. tonsils: **lymphoid tissue on each side of the throat**

4. purulent: **consisting of or discharging pus**

5. discharge: **the flow of fluid from an area of the body; example: a bloody nose**

6. abscess: **swollen area of tissue containing pus**

7. uvula: **fleshy structure that hangs downward in your throat; important functions in speech & swallowing**

8. lymph nodes: **small gland-like masses that filter bacteria and foreign particles; swell when fighting infection**

9. reflexes: **movements made without conscious thought as reactions to stimuli**

10. pyrogen: **the cause of a fever; example: a bacteria**

11. tonsillectomy: **recommended surgical treatment for patients having several episodes of tonsillitis annually**

12. pathogenic: **capable of producing disease**

Investigation 3.4A

Sore Throat

Vocabulary 2: Matching

Directions: Match the definition on the right to the medical term on the left.

1. __C__ erythema

2. __L__ tympanic membrane

3. __H__ tonsils

4. __J__ purulent

5. __D__ discharge

6. __F__ abscess

7. __A__ uvula

8. __K__ lymph nodes

9. __G__ reflexes

10. __E__ pyrogen

11. __B__ tonsillectomy

12. __I__ pathogenic

a. fleshy structure that hangs downward in your throat; important functions in speech & swallowing

b. recommended surgical treatment for patients having several episodes of tonsillitis annually

c. redness of skin or tissue

d. the flow of fluid from an area of the body; example: a bloody nose

e. the cause of a fever; example: a bacteria

f. swollen area of tissue containing pus

g. movements made without conscious thought as reactions to stimuli

h. lymphoid tissue on each side of the throat

i. capable of producing disease

j. consisting of or discharging pus

k. small gland-like masses that filter bacteria and foreign particles; swell when fighting infection

l. thin membrane that separates external and middle ear; vibrates to transmit sound waves

Investigation 3.4A

Sore Throat

Vocabulary 3: Sentences

Directions: Write a complete sentence using each term.

1. erythema: _____

_____

2. tympanic membrane:_____

_____

3. tonsils: _____

_____

4. purulent: _____

_____

5. discharge: _____

_____

6. abscess: _____

_____

7. uvula: _____

_____

8. lymph nodes: _____

_____

9. reflexes: _____

_____

10. pyrogen: _____

_____

11. tonsillectomy: _____

_____

12. pathogenic: _____

_____

Reflections

1. What was your patient's chief complaint?   **Sore Throat**

2. Would you consider Ronald's complaint to be:

   (circle your answer)   **Acute** or Chronic

3. Why?   **Sore throat present four days**

4. How would you classify Ronald's condition (circle your answer)?

   Possible Emergency   or   **Probably Non-Emergency**

5. Which DDx possibilities did you **rule out** right away?

6. a.   **Lymphoma**

   b.   **Carcinoma**

   c.   **Tooth Abscess**

7. Was this an   injury   or   **illness**? (Circle your answer)

8. Was this injury or illness preventable? How or why not? **Probably not. We come in contact with sick people that we don't know are sick often. They cough and breathe in our direction without our permission or knowledge. They put microbes in the air when they breathe and on door handles when they enter the room.**

9. What is the normal range for red blood cells (rbc)?**4.7 - 6.1 million RBC/mcl (microliter)**

10. What is the normal range for white blood cells (wbc)?_**4,500 – 10,000 wbc/mcl**

11. What test would you order to determine their RBC and WBC count? **CBC (Complete Blood Count)**

12. What test is useful to determine which 'bug' is causing an infection?   **Culture, usually done with a Sensitivity test (C&S)**

13. Why might you recommend a tonsillectomy for this patient? **He has suffered with nine or more infections over the past three years. The meets the AMA criteria for recommending a tonsillectomy.**

14. What was your Final Diagnosis? **Acute Tonsillitis with abscessed right tonsil**

15. Why do you think Ronald developed a fever with his throat infection? **He has suffered with nine or more infections over the past three years. The meets the AMA criteria for recommending a tonsillectomy.**

16. What is a "Pyrogen"? **A pyrogen is a protein produced by a bacteria or other organism that produces a reaction in our body that raises the temperature.**

17. How does our body temperature influence the way pathogenic organism grow in our bodies?   **Pathogenic organisms have a narrow temperature range at which they can grow. Most cannot grow above 100 F., so our fever helps our bodies fight infection by limiting their ability to survive.**

Investigation 3.4A   Teacher

Crossword 3.4A   **Sore Throat**

Directions: Use the highlighted terms in the chapter to solve the puzzle. Most clues come from the chapter text, some require outside investigation. Omit spaces or dashes between words.

Solution:

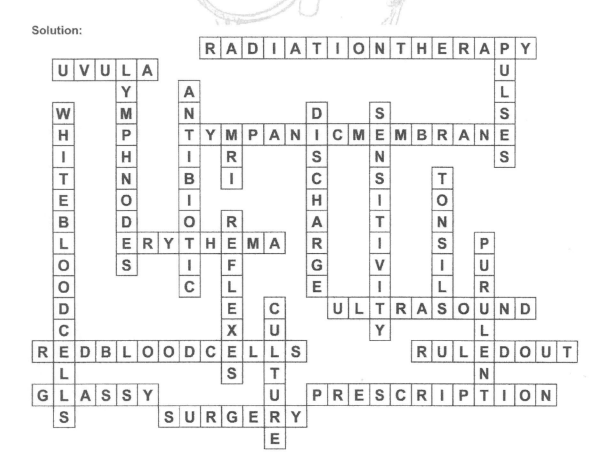

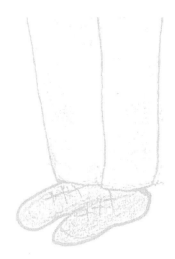

105

Role of Blood

Vocabulary 1: Definitions

Directions: Use the text, a dictionary, or the internet to write a definition for each term.

1. blood: **the liquid that flows in arteries and veins, carrying oxygen and carbon dioxide**

2. plasma: **the liquid component of blood**

3. white blood cells: **lymphocytes, monocytes, basophils, neutrophils, and eosinophils**

4. platelets: **the component of blood that assists in clotting of blood**

5. red blood cells: **hemoglobin-containing cells that carry oxygen and carbon dioxide**

6. centrifuge: **a machine applying centrifugal force to separate fluids of different densities or solids from liquids**

7. suspend: **all blood components spread evenly throughout the blood sample**

8. transfusion: **transfer of blood or its components from one person to another**

9. hemophilia: **hereditary disorder where ability of blood to clot is severely reduced**

10. allergen: **substance causing allergic reaction**

11. hemoglobin: **the component of blood responsible for carrying oxygen**

12. Sickle Cell Anemia: **severe hereditary anemia where red blood cells are crescent shaped**

Role of Blood

Vocabulary 2: Matching

Directions: Match each definition at the right to the medical term on the left.

1. __H__ blood

2. __E__ plasma

3. __A__ white blood cells

4. __J__ platelets

5. __B__ red blood cells

6. __I__ centrifuge

7. __L__ suspend

8. __G__ transfusion

9. __K__ hemophilia

10. __C__ allergen

11. __F__ hemoglobin

12. __D__ Sickle Cell Anemia

a. lymphocytes, monocytes, basophils, neutrophils, and eosinophils

b. hemoglobin-containing cells that carry oxygen and carbon dioxide

c. substance causing allergic reaction

d. severe hereditary anemia where red blood cells are crescent shaped

e. the liquid component of blood

f. the component of blood responsible for carrying oxygen

g. transfer of blood or its components from one person to another

h. the liquid that flows in arteries and veins, carrying oxygen and carbon dioxide

i. a machine applying centrifugal force to separate fluids of different densities or solids from liquids

j. the component of blood that assists in clotting of blood

k. hereditary disorder where ability of blood to clot is severely reduced

l. all blood components spread evenly throughout the blood sample

Investigation 3.4B

Role of Blood

Vocabulary 3: Sentences

Name: _____

Period_____Date_____

Directions: Use the text, a dictionary, or the internet to write a definition for each term.

1. blood: _____

   _____

2. plasma:_____

   _____

3. white blood cells: _____

   _____

4. platelets: _____

   _____

5. red blood cells: _____

   _____

6. centrifuge: _____

   _____

7. suspend: _____

   _____

8. transfusion: _____

   _____

9. hemophilia: _____

   _____

10. allergens: _____

    _____

11. hemoglobin: _____

    _____

12. Sickle Cell Anemia: _____

    _____

Blood Worksheet, page 1   **The Role of Blood**

Directions: Use the information you learned about blood to answer the following questions.

1. What are the three major components of blood?

   a. **plasma**

   b. **platelets and white blood cells**

   c. **red blood cells**

2. What do we call the process by which we stop bleeding when we get a cut?

   Blood clotting or coagulation

3. Which component of blood contains clotting factors?

   Platelets

4. What is the name of the disease where clotting factors are absent?

   Hemophilia

5. What is the liquid part of blood called?

   Plasma

6. List the five types of white blood cells.

   a. **Neutrophils**

   b. **Monocytes**

   c. **Lymphocytes**

   d. **Eosinophils**

   e. **Basophils**

7. Why is it important that we have white blood cells?

   White cells provide our body's defense against infections, toxins, or allergens.

Worksheet 3.4B, Page 2

8. Which white blood cells signal the other cells to attack?

    Eosinophils

9. Which white blood cells are immediately dispatched to fight infection; they are the largest of the white blood cells?

    Monocytes

10. Which white blood cells prevent blood clots from forming too quickly?

    Basophils

11. Which white blood cells provide our main source of 'immunity'?

    Lymphocytes

12. Which white blood cells promote blood flow to the injured area of your body?

    Basophils

13. Which component of blood does NOT need to be tested for blood type compatibility before transfusing into a patient?

    Platelets

14. What is the other name for red blood cells?

    Erythrocytes

15. What component of the red blood cell carries oxygen and carbon dioxide?

    Hemoglobin

Worksheet 3.4B, Page 3

16. Where do red blood cells exchange oxygen for carbon dioxide?

    Tissue Capillaries

17. Why do you think the term 'packed red cells' is used?

    Packed cells are packages of only red cells, which are a solid

18. What should you know about your patient BEFORE giving a transfusion of packed red blood cells?

    My patient's blood type

19. About what percent of your blood is platelets and white blood cells?

    (less than) <1 %

20. In which genetic disease are the red blood cells misshaped such that it is difficult for them to carry oxygen?

    Sickle Cell Anemia

21. Write a paragraph about how Sickle Cell Anemia affects the blood. Research information on the internet and provide evidence from your resources to back up your statements.

    Sometimes children are born with abnormal hemoglobin in their red blood cells. In children born with Sickle Cell Anemia, their red blood cells under certain situations of stress no longer remain round because of their abnormal hemoglobin. If under stress their red cells become elongated they will not pass through capillaries easily and the patient will develop severe pain from lack of oxygen delivery to specific organs or regions of the body.

Art Project: 1. Draw a picture that demonstrates all of the components of blood. 2. Then, draws two red blood cells side by side. The first should be a normal red blood cell and the second a sickled red blood cell. Label every cell in each drawing.

Draw and label all of the components of blood in the box below:

students drawn their interpretations.

Draw a normal RBC on the left. Then draw a sickled RBC on the right.

ROUND

SICKLE-SHAPED

Investigation 3.4B   Teacher

Crossword 3.4B   **Role of Blood**

Directions: Use the highlighted terms in the chapter to solve the puzzle. Most clues come from the chapter text, but some require outside investigation. Omit spaces or dashes between words.

Solution:

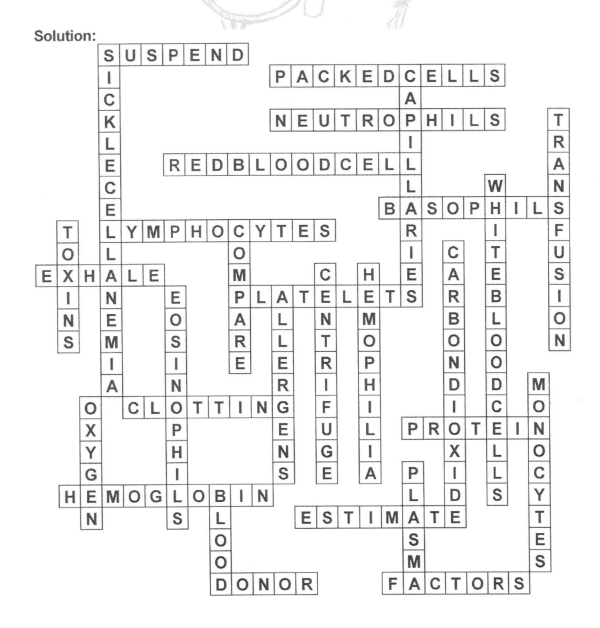

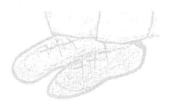

Emergencies

Vocabulary 1: Definitions

Directions: Use the text, a dictionary, or the internet to write a definition for each term.

1. emergency: __any condition requiring immediate treatment to prevent death or
permanent disability__

2. basic life support: __non-invasive emergency procedures to assist immediate survival of
a patient__

3. Red Cross: __organization having mission to care for sick and wounded, and relieve
suffering__

4. CAB: __order of emergency life support: chest compression, airway, breathing__

5. lactic acid: __forms in muscle tissue during strenuous activity__

6. Blood Bank: __a place where blood is stored until needed for transfusion__

7. Scoop and Run: __the concept of getting the injured to the hospital as quickly as
possible without treating in the field__

8. heart attack: __sudden damage to the heart muscle, usually caused by blockage of an
artery within the heart__

9. respiration: __breathing in oxygen and exhaling carbon dioxide__

10. choking: __difficulty breathing due to airway blockage__

11. trachea: __the windpipe that carries oxygen to the lungs__

12. Heimlich Maneuver: __procedure for dislodging an object from a person's windpipe__

Emergencies

Vocabulary 2: Matching

Directions: Match the explanation at the right to the medical term on the left.

1. __C__   emergency

2. __F__   basic life support

3. __G__   Red Cross

4. __J__   CAB

5. __H__   lactic acid

6. __E__   blood bank

7. __A__   scoop and run

8. __B__   heart attack

9. __K__   respiration

10. __I__   choking

11. __L__   trachea

12. __D__   Heimlich Maneuver

a. the concept of getting the injured to the hospital as quickly as possible without treating in the field

b. sudden damage to the heart muscle, usually caused by blockage of an artery within the heart

c. any condition requiring immediate treatment to prevent death or permanent disability

d. procedure for dislodging an object from a person's windpipe

e. a place where blood is stored until needed for transfusion

f. non-invasive emergency procedures to assist immediate survival of a patient

g. organization having mission to care for sick and wounded, and relieve suffering

h. forms in muscle tissue during strenuous activity

i. difficulty breathing due to airway blockage

j. order of emergency life support: chest compression, airway, breathing

k. breathing in oxygen and exhaling carbon dioxide

l. the windpipe that carries oxygen to the lungs

Emergencies

Vocabulary 3: Sentences

Directions: Use each term in a sentence.

1. emergency: _____

_____

2. basic life support:_____

_____

3. Red Cross: _____

_____

4. CAB: _____

_____

5. lactic acid: _____

_____

6. Blood Bank: _____

_____

7. Scoop and Run: _____

_____

8. heart attack: _____

_____

9. respiration: _____

_____

10. choking: _____

_____

11. trachea: _____

_____

12. Heimlich Maneuver: _____

_____

Investigation 3.5A – Emergencies   Teacher

Emergencies Worksheet

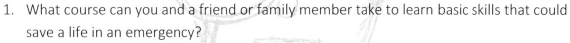

1. What course can you and a friend or family member take to learn basic skills that could save a life in an emergency?
   Basic Life Support

2. Name two organizations who sponsor Basic Life Support training that you can contact to schedule a class?

   a. **American Heart Association**
   b. **Red Cross**

3. What is the first thing you should do when coming upon an obvious medical emergency?
   Get Help

4. What do the letters CAB stand for in the order of basic life support?

   a. **Circulation**
   b. **Airway**
   c. **Breathing**

5. When your body produces energy while you are unable to breath, what toxic chemical accumulates in your blood?
   lactic acid

6. If you come upon a non-responsive person lying on the ground and you cannot detect a pulse, what is the first thing you should do after calling 911?
   vigorous chest compressions to keep the blood moving

7. Should you come upon a person who is bleeding profusely, what can you do to help keep them from bleeding to death?
   apply pressure to the bleeding area

8. Basic Life Support classes teach you how to respond when you come upon someone suffering from what possible scenarios:

    a. heart attack

    b. stroke

    c. choking

    d. loss of breathing

    e. severe bleeding

9. If you are visiting your grandmother and she suffers a sudden loss of her vision, speech, or sudden muscle weakness, what should you do?

    get her to the emergency room as soon as possible

10. In the above situation, what might be happening to your grandmother?

    she might be having a stroke

11. What is the "time window" to get a stroke victim to a hospital to give the best chance of survival with the least long-term disability?

    less than three hours

12. When someone is brought to the emergency room with severe bleeding, what is the emergency doctor likely to order?

    send the patient to surgery, followed by blood transfusion

13. Where does the emergency room get blood for transfusions?

    the blood bank

14. When someone at the dinner table suddenly cannot talk and grabs their throat, what is probably happening?

   they are probably choking from food blocking their airway

15. What is the medical term for "wind pipe"?

   trachea

16. What is the name of the technique used to expel food lodged in the wind pipe by squeezing the victim's abdomen?

   Heimlich maneuver

17. Why do choking victims never yell for help?

   no air can escape from their throat to make a sound

18. Why is the term "Heart Attack" an inadequate explanation of a heart problem?

   the term "Heart Attack" is not specific to one heart problem

19. What is a 'Myocardial Infarction"?

   where blood supply to part of heart is blocked, causing death of those heart muscle cells

20. Which sensors located in the heart recognize an inadequate oxygen supply and cause a reduction in blood flow to non-vital organs?

   ischemia receptors

21. What is ventricular fibrillation?

    where the heart muscle cells get out of rhythm, so it no longer pumps blood in its

    normal efficient manner

22. What can be done to help a person suffering ventricular fibrillation?

    apply an electrical stimulus using a defibrillator to restore normal rhythm

23. How would you know how to use a defibrillator you find and need to use at school if no

    adult is around?

    the defibrillator has a voice track that tells you what to do

    _____

24. If someone in your home experiences sudden chest pain spreading into their left arm or

    their jaw, what should you do?

    get them to the emergency room as soon as possible

    Why? **They could be having a myocardial infarction**

25. Do you need to be 21 years old to become certified in Basic Life Support?

    NO   YES   (circle your choice)

26. How is myocardial infarction different from ventricular fibrillation? (2 ways)

    a. **M.I. caused by blockage of artery; V-Fib caused by loss of hear rhythm**

    b. **In ventricular fibrillation there is no chest pain, just suddenly no pulse. In**

       myocardial infarction there is severe chest pain and abnormal pulse

Crossword   **Emergencies**

Directions: Use the highlighted terms in the chapter to solve the puzzle. Most clues come from the chapter text, some require outside investigation. Omit spaces or dashes between words.

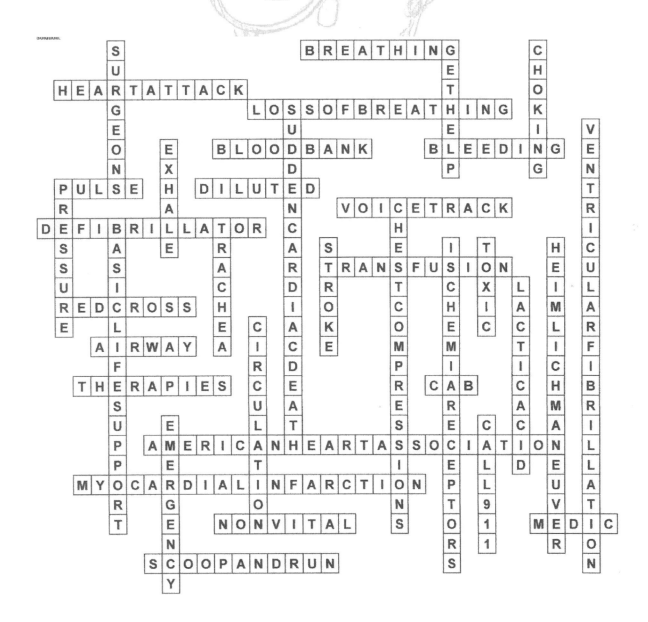

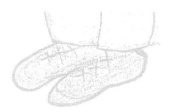

Chest Pain

Vocabulary 1: Definitions

Directions: Use the text, a dictionary, or the internet to write a definition for each term.

a. myocardial infarction: __death of heart muscle tissue occurring in a heart attack__

b. angina: __acute chest pain caused by inadequate heart blood supply__

c. aortic dissection: __tearing of the inner layer of aorta__

d. pericarditis: __inflammation of the outer covering of the heart__

e. radiates: __pain that spreads away from the starting point__

f. costochondritis: __inflammation of the cartilage connecting the ribs to the sternum__

g. cartilage: __strong, bendable tissue found in your nose and external ears, also lines joints__

h. pleurisy: __inflammation of the outer covering of the lungs__

i. inspiration: __breathing in air__

j. collapsed lung: __buildup of air between lung and chest wall causing progressive breathing difficulty__

k. panic attack: __sudden feeling of disabling anxiety__

l. shingles: __painful condition stimulated by re-activation of chicken pox virus years later__

Chest Pain

Vocabulary 2: Matching

Directions: Match the definitions on the right to the medical terms on the left.

a. sudden feeling of disabling anxiety

b. tearing of the inner layer of aorta

1. __H__ myocardial infarction

c. breathing in air

2. __F__ angina

d. pain that spreads away from the
starting point

3. __B__ aortic dissection

4. __L__ pericarditis

e. strong, bendable tissue found in
your nose and external ears, also
lines joints

5. __D__ radiates

6. __G__ costochondritis

f. acute chest pain caused by
inadequate heart blood supply

7. __E__ cartilage

g. inflammation of the cartilage
connecting the ribs to the sternum

8. __J__ pleurisy

9. __C__ inspiration

h. death of heart muscle tissue
occurring in a heart attack

10. __I__ collapsed lung

i. buildup of air between lung and
chest wall causing progressive
breathing difficulty

11. __A__ panic attack

12. __K__ shingles

j. inflammation of the outer covering
of the lungs

k. painful condition stimulated by re-
activation of chicken pox virus years
later

l. inflammation of the outer covering
of the heart

Chest Pain

Vocabulary 3: Sentences

Directions: Write a sentence using each term.

1. myocardial infarction: _____

_____

2. angina: _____

_____

3. aortic dissection: _____

_____

4. pericarditis: _____

_____

5. radiates: _____

_____

6. costochondritis: _____

_____

7. cartilage: _____

_____

8. pleurisy: _____

_____

9. inspiration (medical use): _____

_____

10. collapsed lung: _____

_____

11. panic attack: _____

_____

12. shingles (not on a roof): _____

_____

Chest Pain Worksheet

Chest Pain Worksheet

1. True or **False**: In well over half of all emergency room visits for chest pain the final diagnosis is "myocardial infarction".

2. Name five major categories of chest pain:

   a. **Heart**
   b. **Digestive**
   c. **Bone and muscle**
   d. **Lung**
   e. **Other**

3. Name four causes of cardiac chest pain:

   a. **Myocardial infarction**
   b. **Angina**
   c. **Aortic dissection**
   d. **Pericarditis**

4. What is a myocardial infarction?

   Death of an area of the heart caused by restricted blood flow

5. What is Angina?

   Chest pain caused by reduced cardiac blood flow

6. What causes patients to feel Angina?

   Ischemic Receptors

Chest Pain Worksheet , P.2

7. What is Aortic Dissection?

    A rupture of the aorta, which can result in sudden death

8. What is the pericardium?

    Outer protective membrane of the heart

9. What is pericarditis?

    Inflammation or infection of the pericardium

10. Why is pericarditis a dangerous condition?

    The heart's ability to pump blood can be impeded

11. What does the esophagus connect?

    Mouth and stomach

12. What causes heartburn?

    Stomach acid backwashes and burns inside of esophagus

13. Why do disorders of the gall bladder and pancreas cause chest pain?

    Migration of gall bladder and pancreas from chest in human development; brain still perceives nerve impulses as though still in chest

Chest Pain Worksheet , P.3

14. Costochondritis represents injury to what body structure(s)?

   Cartilage joining ribs to sternum

15. Which other major organ is located in the chest?

   Lungs

16. What is a pulmonary embolism?

   Blood clot or other material get lodged in a lung artery, making gas exchange in lung difficult

17. What complication can occur in the presence of pulmonary hypertension?

   Fluid can accumulate in lungs

18. During which part of the respiratory cycle is pain caused in Pleurisy?

   Inspiration

19. Name two non-specific origins of chest pain:

   a. **Panic attack**
   b. **Shingles**

20. What technique does an emergency room doctor use to make the diagnosis on a patient with chest pain?

   Rule out potential causes until valid explanation remains

Dr._____

P.____Date_____

21. Write a paragraph about someone in your family who experienced chest pain or visited the emergency room for another reason. Write your impressions of their experience.

_____

_____

_____

_____

_____

_____

_____

_____

_____

_____

_____

_____

_____

_____

_____

_____

_____

_____

_____

_____

_____

_____

Investigation 3.5B   Teacher

Crossword 3.5B   **Chest Pain**

Directions: Use the highlighted terms in the chapter to solve the puzzle. Most clues come from the chapter text, some require outside investigation. Omit spaces or dashes between words.

Solution:

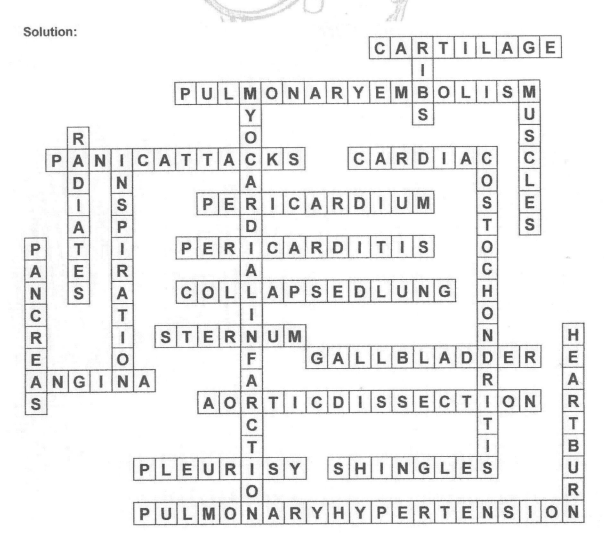

Chronic Disease

Vocabulary 1: Definitions

Directions: Use the text, a dictionary, or the internet to write a definition for each term.

1. obesity: **severely overweight; a huge problem associated with over-eating**

2. carbohydrates: **food group that includes sugars and starches; includes potatoes, pasta, bread, candy**

3. protein: **essential long chains of amino acids; examples include hair and finger/toenails**

4. fat: **adipose tissue; typically stored beneath skin or around organs**

5. type II diabetes: **chronic condition where insulin is made, but not utilized efficiently**

6. consultation: **an examination performed at the request of another physician**

7. percussion (as used in a medical examination): **examination technique using tapping to determine size, texture, and shape of organs**

8. bowel sounds: **normal grumbling sounds from the abdomen caused by peristalsis**

9. distention: **enlarged or swollen from too much internal pressure**

10. hemoglobin A1C: **test that determines average blood sugar concentrations over 2 to 3 months**

11. type 1 diabetes: **chronic condition where pancreas produces little or no insulin**

12. genetic abnormality: **congenital problem caused by abnormality within the genes**

Investigation 3.6A

Chronic Disease

Vocabulary 2: Matching

Directions: Match the definitions on the right to the terms on the left.

1. __E___ obesity

2. __I___ carbohydrates

3. __A___ protein

4. __D___ fat

5. __L___ type II diabetes

6. __K___ consultation

7. __F___ percussion

8. __J___ bowel sounds

9. __B___ distention

10. __G___ hemoglobin A1C

11. __C___ type 1 diabetes

12. __H___ genetic abnormality

a. essential long chains of amino acids; examples include hair and finger/toenails

b. enlarged or swollen from too much internal pressure

c. chronic condition where pancreas produces little or no insulin

d. adipose tissue; typically stored beneath skin or around organs

e. severely overweight; a huge problem associated with over-eating

f. examination technique using tapping to determine size, texture, and shape of organs

g. test that determines average blood sugar concentrations over 2 to 3 months

h. congenital problem caused by abnormality within the genes

i. food group that includes sugars and starches; includes potatoes, pasta, bread, candy

j. normal grumbling sounds from the abdomen caused by peristalsis

k. an examination performed at the request of another physician

l. chronic condition where insulin is made, but not utilized efficiently

Investigation 3.6A

Chronic Disease

Vocabulary 3: Sentences

Directions: Write a sentence using each word.

1. obesity: _____

_____

2. carbohydrates:_____

_____

3. protein: _____

_____

4. fat: _____

_____

5. type II diabetes: _____

_____

6. consultation: _____

_____

7. percussion: _____

_____

8. bowel sounds: _____

_____

9. distention: _____

_____

10. hemoglobin A1C: _____

_____

11. type 1 diabetes: _____

_____

12. genetic abnormality: _____

_____

Worksheet 3.6A

   Title: Diabetes Workup

Directions: Use the information from your reading to complete your diabetes workup on this patient.

Patient Name: **Gilbert Isaacs**   Age: **72**   Gender: **M** F

Vital Signs: **Ht**: **71 in Wt: 188** lbs   **BP: 132 / 89** mmHg   **Pulse: 22** b/m Temp: **98.6°** F

CC: Referred for diabetic control in preparation for left knee replacement surgery

HxCC: (List important information from patient in history of chief complaint)

   1. **referred for implant L knee**

   2. **Type II diabetes, non-controlled**

   3. **Hemoglobin A1C = 7.8%**

ROS: (List all positive findings from Review of Records)- list additional positives on back)

   1. **history of obesity (270 pounds)**

   2. **history of nocturia (frequent night time urination) with rapid weight loss**

Positive Examination Findings:

   1. **vision corrected by trifocals**

   2. **partial dentures**

   3. **enlarged left knee with decreased range of motion**

   4. **pain upon flexion or extension of left and right knees**

DDX:

   1. **Type II diabetes, not currently well controlled**

   2. **Arthritis L > R knee**

   3. **needs L knee implant**

Place an 'X' on the line next to any test you would consider at this time to help your investigation of this patient's medical problem. Write <u>NA</u> for any test listed that is probably not appropriate to your evaluation of this condition:

_____	X-rays of abdomen including pancreas and liver
_____	Complete Blood Count (CBC)
_____	MRI of the pancreas and liver
_____	Ultrasound of Pancreas and Liver
X	Repeat A1C blood test

Lab Test Results:

The following chart represents the key to reading Hemoglobin A1C test results:

Diabetes Diagnosis	Hemoglobin A1C level in blood
Normal (non-diabetic)	Less than (<) 5.7%
Pre-diabetic	Between 5.7% and 6.4%
Diabetes	6.5% or greater
Gilbert's 2nd A1C results	****7.7%****

A1C Lab Test Difference: What are some possible explanations as to the difference between the A1C test ordered by Dr. Drazer and the second test ordered by you?

1. **each doctor may have used a different lab for the test**

2. **patient may have altered his diet**

3. **patient may have changed his medication regimen**

Diagnosis. (Hint: Find them on the DDX list)

1. **non-controlled type II diabetes**

2. **arthritic left knee for implant surgery**

Treatment Recommendations: What is the order of progressive treatment for Type II Diabetes?

1. **strict diet management**

2. **increase physical activity (as tolerated)**

3. **proper medication and dosage**

Check the appropriate box to indicate how this medical condition spreads from one person to another (more than one method of spreading may exist):

Method of spreading	yes	no
Through the air		X
Skin to skin contact with another person		X
Touching contaminated object		X
Genetic sharing within families	X	
Contact with contaminated blood		X
Drinking contaminated water		X
Contact with contaminated urine		X
Cannot be spread to friends	X	

Interview someone you know who has diabetes. Are they related to you? From your observations do they look any different from others you know who are not diabetic? What type of diabetes do they have and what is their treatment regimen? How has having diabetes changed their life? What do they do to keep their diabetes under control? (Continue on back of page if needed)

_____

_____

_____

_____

_____

_____

_____

_____

_____

_____

_____

Page 4

Reflections:

1. What was your patient's (Gilbert) chief complaint?

    pain left knee

    non-controlled type II diabetes (referring physician complaint)

2. Would you consider Gilbert's complaint to be: (circle) Acute or **Chronic**

    Why? **type II diabetes is a chronic medical condition that can be controlled, but usually does not go away.**

3. How would you classify Gilbert's condition (circle your answer)?

    Possible Emergency   or   **Probably Non-Emergency**

4. Was this an injury or **illness**? (Circle your answer)

5. Was this injury or illness preventable? How or why not?

The lifestyle choices that often cause type II diabetes are preventable by making better diet, activity, and other lifestyle choices. We cannot control genetic factors that may influence the occurrence of type II diabetes.

6. What is considered the normal range for an A1C blood test?   **<5.7%**

7. List some of the symptoms Gilbert exhibited before he was diagnosed as having diabetes.

    a. **obesity (270 lbs)**

    b. **nocturia (frequent night time urination)**

    c. **rapid weight loss**

    d. **excessive thirst**

8. What test would you order to determine if your patient is normal, pre-diabetic, or diabetic? **either a glucose tolerance test or hemoglobin A1C test**

9. What is happening within the body in Type I Diabetes?

    Islet cells of the pancreas cannot produce adequate amounts of insulin.

10. What is happening within the body in Type II Diabetes?

    In type II diabetes the pancreas continues manufacturing insulin, but the body is

    ineffective in absorbing the glucose from the bloodstream.

11. How many types of Diabetes have been identified to date?   **five**

12. Do you think Gilbert's weight of 270 pounds before he developed Type II Diabetes could
    have been a factor in his current left knee condition? How?

    Yes Carrying extra weight day in and day out causes extra stress on the weight

    bearing joints, especially the knees.

13. Which of the following are questions that should have been asked of Gilbert during his
    first visit back to your office following his referral from Dr. Drazer? (put an 'X' beside
    each appropriate question)

    a. _____ Have you had your knee implant surgery yet?

    b. __**X**__ Have you changed your diet recently?

    c. _____ Is your knee feeling better with the medicine I gave you?

    d. __**X**__ Have you been taking your diabetic medicine regularly and in the
        correct dose?

    e. _____ Have you checked your blood pressure at home recently?

    f. _____ Have you noticed a lump on your pancreas recently?

Dr:_____

14. Write about the known effects of diabetes on the human body. Use your current knowledge and the internet to research the topic.

_____

_____

_____

_____

_____

_____

_____

_____

_____

_____

_____

_____

_____

_____

_____

_____

_____

_____

_____

_____

Diabetes

Vocabulary 1: Definitions

Directions: Use the text, a dictionary, or the internet to write a definition for each term.

1. diabetes: __chronic disease where pancreas produces too little insulin or insulin__

2. culture (as used medically): __growing bacteria to determine its identity and which antibiotic will be effective__

3. preventable: __an unnecessary illness or injury__

4. complications: __side effects or undesirable outcomes of treatment or recovery from an injury or illness__

5. neuropathy: __diminished sensitivity of peripheral nerves caused by injury or disease__

6. retinopathy: __injury or disease of retina resulting in loss of or diminished vision__

7. gangrene: __death of tissue from lack of blood supply__

8. hemorrhage: __heavy discharge of blood from an artery or vein__

9. ophthalmoscope: __instrument for examining the interior of the eye, especially the retina__

10. Islets of Langerhans: __the area of the pancreas where insulin is produced__

11. alpha cells: __pancreatic cells that produce glucagon__

12. beta cells: __pancreatic cells that produce insulin__

Teacher

Vocabulary 2: Matching

Directions: Match the definitions on the right to the medical terms on the left.

1. __D__ diabetes

2. __J__ culture

3. __F__ preventable

4. __B__ complications

5. __K__ neuropathy

6. __H__ retinopathy

7. __E__ gangrene

8. __L__ hemorrhage

9. __A__ ophthalmoscope

10. __I__ Islets of Langerhans

11. __C__ alpha cells

12. __G__ beta cells

a. instrument for examining the interior of the eye, especially the retina

b. side effects or undesirable outcomes of treatment or recovery from an injury or illness

c. pancreatic cells that produce glucagon

d. chronic disease where pancreas produces too little insulin or insulin not effectively utilized

e. death of tissue from lack of blood supply

f. an unnecessary illness or injury

g. the type of pancreatic cells that produce insulin

h. injury or disease of retina resulting in loss of or diminished vision

i. the area of the pancreas where insulin is produced

j. growing bacteria to determine its identity and which antibiotic will be effective

k. diminished sensitivity of peripheral nerves caused by injury or disease

l. heavy discharge of blood from an artery or vein

Name: _____

Diabetes

Period_____Date_____

Vocabulary 3: Sentences

Directions: Write a complete sentence using each word.

1. diabetes: _____

   _____

2. culture: _____

   _____

3. preventable: _____

   _____

4. complications: _____

   _____

5. neuropathy: _____

   _____

6. retinopathy: _____

   _____

7. gangrene: _____

   _____

8. hemorrhage: _____

   _____

9. ophthalmoscope: _____

   _____

10. Islets of Langerhans: _____

   _____

11. alpha cells: _____

   _____

12. beta cells: _____

   _____

Worksheet 1: Diabetes

Diabetes

1. What is diabetes?

Diabetes is a chronic, mostly preventable disease where insulin is not produced or glucose is not effectively utilized, resulting in elevated blood glucose levels.

2. What percent of the American population suffers from diabetes?

    ~ 25%

3. Does one's culture have the potential to affect their risk of developing type 2 diabetes? (Circle your answer) **YES** NO   In what ways? (describe below)

    Our cultural background can effect our diet and physical forms of activity, both of which can impact our chances of developing diabetes.

4. Is the occurrence of Diabetes in the United States increasing or decreasing?

    increasing

5. What other disturbing health occurrence that affects the rates of diabetes has an upward trend in the United States?

    increasing trend in obesity

6. Is type 1 diabetes preventable? Yes **No**

7. Is type 2 diabetes generally preventable? **Yes** No

8. What is the number one factor in the upward trend of diabetes? **obesity**

9. What are the two most important factors in the upward trend in obesity?

    a. **diet**

    b. **diminishing amount of physical activity**

10. List <u>five</u> things a patient can do to reduce their risk of diabetes.

    a. **regular health care**

    b. **limit sugar intact**

    c. **reduce weight**

    d. **increase exercise or physical activity**

    e. **reduce stress**

11. What is the number one influence on a person's diet? **ethnicity**

12. Describe how physicians are also teachers.

> **Doctors spend a great deal of time educating their patients about how to live**
>
> **a healthier life.**

13. Name seven or more complications that attack your diabetic patient's health.

   1. **depression**
   2. **retinopathy**
   3. **cerebrovascular disease**
   4. **heart disease**
   5. **kidney disease_**
   6. **peripheral neuropathy**
   7. **peripheral vascular disease**
   8. **skin ulcers**
   9. **gangrene**

14. Which two hormones produced in the pancreas regulate your body's blood sugar levels?

   insulin and glucagon

15. What is the basic function of insulin? **Insulin lowers blood glucose levels**

16. What is the basic function of glucagon? **glucagon raises blood glucose levels**

17. In which pancreatic cells are insulin and glucagon produced? **Glucose is produced in the beta cells of the Islets of Langerhans, while glucagon is produced in the alpha cells of the Islets of Langerhans.**

18. Where within the abdominal cavity is the pancreas located?

   The pancreas is located mostly under the stomach

19. What medical instrument is useful to evaluate the condition of your diabetic patient's retina?

   ophthalmoscope

Worksheet 3.6B2: Diabetes   **Vocabulary Match**

Directions: Place the letter of the definition in the space provided on the left of the medical term.

1. __J__   Diabetes

2. __E__   Ethnicity

3. __O__   Preventable

4. __G__   Dietary practices

5. __A__   Complications

6. __D__   Preventive measures

7. __Q__   Educator

8. __L__   Glucose

9. __R__   Capillary

10. __N__   Neuropathy

11. __P__   Retinopathy

12. __F__   Gangrene

13. __C__   Retina

14. __H__   Hemorrhages

15. __K__   Regulate

16. __I__   Islets of Langerhans

17. __M__   Insulin

18. __B__   glucagon

a. Problems that arise during an illness or from the treatment that add to your patient's suffering.

b. Hormone produced in pancreas that indirectly raises blood sugar

c. Structure of the eye where the image seen is focused

d. Things you and your patients can do to prevent illness

e. Your family heritage, based on your ancestors

f. Black tissue that is dead from infection or lack of blood supply

g. The things you choose to eat

h. When blood leaks out of capillaries and other blood vessels

i. The cells in the pancreas where insulin is produced

j. A disease where the body does not maintain a proper balance of blood glucose

k. The ability to control, such as maintaining the appropriate blood glucose range

l. The medical name for sugar when it is in the blood

m. The hormone produced in the pancreas responsible for lowering blood sugar

n. When the sensory or motor nerves have diminished function

o. Things you can stop before they happen

p. When the capillaries in the back of the eye leak blood onto the retina

q. You, as a doctor, are also a teacher or _(synonym)_

r. Very small blood vessels where oxygen and nutrients enter cells

Investigation 3.6B - Diabetes   Teacher

Worksheet 3.6B3: Diabetic Complications

Directions: Write the name of each <u>diabetic complication</u> in the space provided next to its number from the diagram.

1. __**kidney disease**__

2. __**cerebrovascular disease**__

3. __**skin ulcers**__

4. __**retinopathy**__

5. __**peripheral vascular disease**__

6. __**heart disease**__

7. __**gangrene**__

8. __**depression**__

9. __**peripheral neuropathy**__

10. __**periodontal disease**__

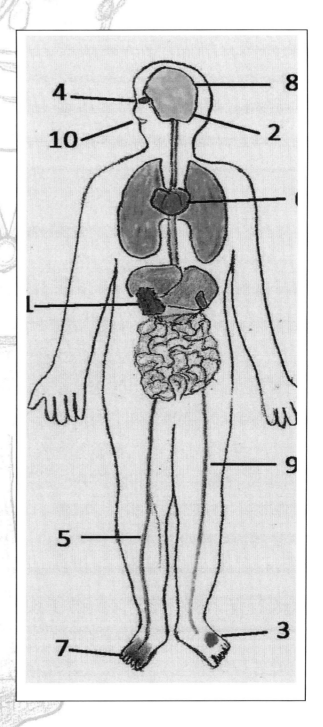

Worksheet 3.6B4: Abdominal Organs

Directions: Write the name of each abdominal organ in the space provided next to its number from the diagram.

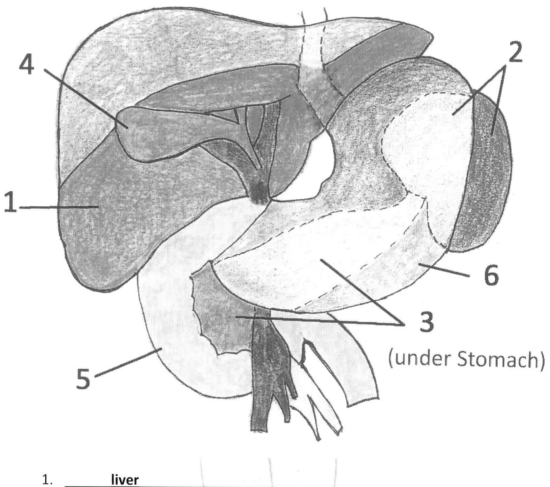

1. _____liver_____

2. _____kidney_____

3. _____pancreas_____

4. _____gallbladder_____

5. _____duodenum_____

6. _____stomach_____

Investigation 3.6A/B   Teacher

Crossword   Chronic Disease: Diabetes

Directions: Use the highlighted terms in the chapter to solve the puzzle. Most clues come from the chapter text, some require outside investigation. Omit spaces or dashes between words.

Solution:

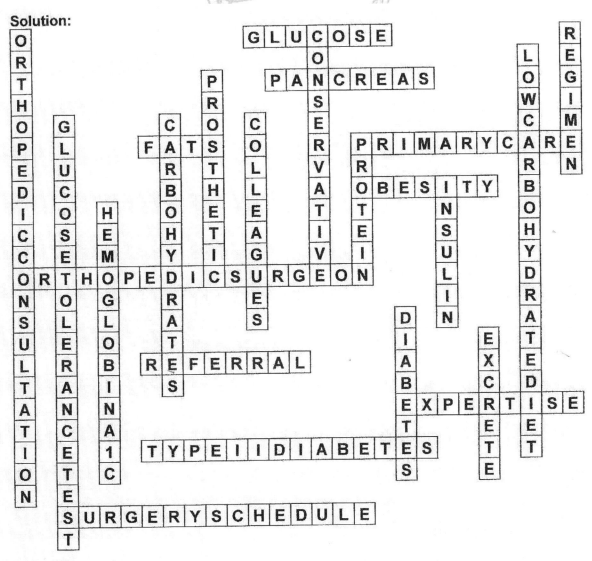

Shoulder Pain

Vocabulary 1: Definitions

Directions: Use the text, a dictionary, or the internet to write a definition for each term.

1. precipitate: **anything that causes something else to happen**

2. anti-inflammatory: **medicine that stops or prevents inflammation from happening**

3. modalities: **available treatments for an illness or injury**

4. pain scale: **a rating scale describing the degree of pain felt**

5. cyst: **abnormal membrane-bordered sac containing semi-liquid material**

6. hypertension: **elevated blood pressure**

7. osseous: **pertaining to bone**

8. mobilization: **making a joint move or moveable**

9. crepitus: **grating sensation or sound from movement of severely arthritic joints**

10. splinting: **tightening surrounding muscles to not moving an area to prevent pain and protect the injured area**

11. edema: **swelling of an area of tissue or around a joint**

12. erythema: **redness of tissue overlying and area of inflammation or infection**

Shoulder Pain

Vocabulary 2: Matching

Directions: Match the definitions on the right to the medical terms on the left.

1. __F__ precipitate

2. __E__ anti-inflammatory

3. __H__ modalities

4. __C__ pain scale

5. __L__ cyst

6. __D__ hypertension

7. __K__ osseous

8. __A__ mobilization

9. __J__ crepitus

10. __I__ splinting

11. __B__ edema

12. __G__ erythema

a. making a joint move or moveable

b. swelling of an area of tissue or around a joint

c. a rating scale describing the degree of pain felt

d. elevated blood pressure

e. medicine that stops or prevents inflammation

f. anything that causes something else to happen

g. redness of tissue overlying and area of inflammation or infection

h. available treatments for an illness or injury

i. tightening surrounding muscles to not moving an area to prevent pain and protect the injured area

j. grating sensation or sound from movement of severely arthritic joints

k. pertaining to bone

l. abnormal membrane-bordered sac containing semi-liquid material

Investigation 3.7A

Shoulder Pain

Vocabulary 3: Sentences

Directions: Write a sentence using each vocabulary term.

1. precipitate: _____

_____

2. anti-inflammatory: _____

_____

3. modalities: _____

_____

4. pain scale: _____

_____

5. cyst: _____

_____

6. hypertension: _____

_____

7. osseous: _____

_____

8. mobilization: _____

_____

9. crepitus: _____

_____

10. splinting: _____

_____

11. edema: _____

_____

12. erythema: _____

_____

Dr. _____

P. _____ Date _____

Orthopedic Worksheet

1. Would you consider referring George to another physician to treat his shoulder?

    Yes   No

2. If yes, to which physician specialist would you refer George?

    Orthopedist

3. If you decided to continue this patient under your care for the immediate future, to which part of the physician support team might you refer George?

    physical therapist

4. Assuming you referred your patient to an Orthopedist having sub-specialty training, which specialist would best serve this patient's needs?

    shoulder or upper extremity orthopedic specialist

5. Perhaps your interest in medicine leans more toward healing injuries than curing illness? Take this opportunity to research the training time required to enter the field of Orthopedic Surgery.

    a. Number of years undergraduate college education =   __4__

    b. Number of years of medical school education =   __4__

    c. Number of years Orthopedic Residency Training =   __5__

    d. Total number of years of college + medical training =   __13__

    e. Can an orthopedist become a sub-specialist with additional training?   No, that's it.   **<u>Yes</u>**

6. List and define three classifications of injury based on duration of symptoms:

    A. acute – occurring within the last few days

    B. sub-acute – occurring within a few weeks to months

    C. chronic – first occurring months or longer ago

7. List ten surgical procedures performed by Orthopedic Surgeons.

    a. **closed reduction of a displaced fracture**

    b. **open reduction of a displaced fracture**

    c. **excision and curettage of infected bone and tissue**

    d. **bone biopsy for suspected bone cancer**

    e. **re-attach torn muscles or ligaments**

    f. **total joint replacement of hip, shoulder, knee, or ankle**

    g. **repair torn rotator cuff of shoulder**

    h. **ligament repair of elbow**

    i. **arthroscopic surgery of knee**

    j. **ligament replacement or repair of knee**

8. List four types of non-surgical treatment provided by Orthopedists.

    a. **apply plaster or fiberglass casts or splints**

    b. **injections of local anesthetic or steroids**

    c. **physical mobilization or traction treatment**

    d. **Prescribe oral medications**

9. Name and describe two serious injuries commonly suffered by baseball pitchers.

    a. **repair of torn rotator cuff and labrum of shoulder**

    b. **repair torn ligaments of elbow**

10. Name <u>two</u> reasons an Orthopedic Surgeon might decide to operate on a patient.

    a. **repair of a displaced fracture requiring internal fixation**

    b. **repair of torn ligaments, muscles, or cartilage**

    c. **clean out infected bone**

Crossword 3.7A   **Shoulder Pain**   P.____Date:_____

Directions: Use the highlighted terms in the chapter to solve the puzzle. Most clues come from the chapter text, some require outside investigation. Omit spaces or dashes between words.

Solution:

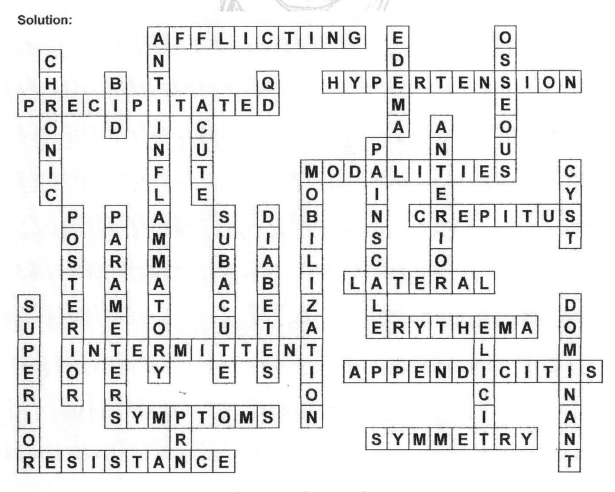

Joints

Vocabulary 1: Definitions

Directions: Use the text, a dictionary, or the internet to write a definition for each term.

1. ball and socket: **joint allowing multi-directional movement and rotation**

2. hinge: **the type of joint that moves like a door, such as your elbow**

3. flexion: **bending a joint, such as your knee**

4. extension: **straightening of a joint, such as your elbow**

5. ligament: **structures that connect bone to bone**

6. muscles: **tissues providing the power to move joints, attached to bones by tendons**

7. fusion: **when two osseous surfaces join to together such that no movement occurs**

8. joint: **any place where two bones meet, regardless of the type of motion allowed**

9. synovial fluid: **lubricating liquid material that assists smooth movement of joints**

10. articulating cartilage: **the white, smooth surface of a normal joint where two bones are joined**

11. osteoarthritis: **destruction of a joint due to wear and tear over several years**

12. rheumatoid arthritis: **chronic progressive disease causing joint inflammation, pain, and immobility**

Investigation 3.7B

Joints

Vocabulary 2: Matching

Directions: Match the definitions at the right to the medical terms on the left.

1. __A__ ball and socket

2. __J__ hinge

3. __H__ flexion

4. __D__ extension

5. __L__ ligament

6. __G__ muscles

7. __E__ fusion

8. __C__ joint

9. __B__ synovial fluid

10. __I__ articulating cartilage

11. __K__ osteoarthritis

12. __F__ rheumatoid arthritis

a. joint allowing multi-directional movement and rotation

b. lubricating liquid material that assists smooth movement of joints

c. any place where two bones meet, regardless of the type of motion allowed

d. straightening of a joint, such as your elbow

e. when two osseous surfaces join to together such that no movement occurs

f. chronic progressive disease causing joint inflammation, pain, and immobility

g. tissues providing the power to move joints, attached to bones by tendons

h. bending a joint, such as your knee

i. the white, smooth surface of a normal joint where two bones are joined

j. the type of joint that moves like a door, such as your elbow

k. destruction of a joint due to wear and tear over several years

l. structures that connect bone to bone

Investigation 3.7B

Joints

Vocabulary 3: Sentences

Dr. _____

P._____Date_____

Directions: Use each term below in a sentence.

1. ball and socket: _____

   _____

2. hinge:_____

   _____

3. flexion: _____

   _____

4. extension: _____

   _____

5. ligament: _____

   _____

6. muscles: _____

   _____

7. fusion: _____

   _____

8. joint: _____

   _____

9. synovial fluid: _____

   _____

10. articulating cartilage: _____

   _____

11. osteoarthritis: _____

   _____

12. rheumatoid arthritis: _____

   _____

Investigation 3.7B: Joints

Worksheet 1: Joints

Joints Worksheet

Directions: Answer the following questions about joints. You may refer to your previous reading in this section.

1. What is a joint? **the place where two bones come together; where movement occurs**

2. Name three types of joints according to their degree and range of motion.

    a. **ball and socket joint: allows motion in many directions and angles**

    b. **hinge joint: permits motion in one plane, flexion & extension**

    c. **slightly moveable or non-moveable: permits little or no motion**

3. Describe the action of a ball and socket joint. **allows motion at many angles and ranges.**

4. Give an example of a ball and socket joint in humans. **shoulder or hip joints**

5. Provide a non-human example of a ball and socket joint. **adjustable lamp** or any other example

6. Describe the action of a hinge joint. **Allows motion in a single plane with limited range**

7. Provide an example of a hinge joint found on the human body.

    Hinge joints are found in the elbows and knees, and fingers and toes

8. Think of a non-human hinge joint and write it below.

    a hinged door

9. Provide an example of slightly moveable joints in humans. **spinal bones**

10. What structure encompasses (encloses) a joint? **joint capsule**

11. What connects the bones across a joint? **ligaments**

12. What structure powers bones and joints to move? **muscles**

13. Name two structures that allow smooth movement of a joint and protect it from wearing out:

    a. **articulating cartilage**

    b. **synovial fluid**

Worksheet 1: Joints, page 2

14. Give an example of slightly moveable joints in your body.

   bones within the wrist, bones of the skull, bones of the spine

15. What disease occurs in older people when the smooth sliding surfaces of their joints wear out? **Osteoarthritis**

16. What disease occurs in young and older people where their immune system attacks joints within their own body? **Rheumatoid Arthritis**

17. Place your dominant hand on top of your head touching the top of your ear on the other side. Keep it there for five minutes by the clock while you straighten up your room or help out in the kitchen. Write a paragraph about your experience not having the use of your arm. What simple things could you no longer do?

_____

_____

_____

_____

_____

_____

_____

_____

_____

_____

_____

_____

_____

_____

_____

Crossword   **Joints**

Directions: Use the highlighted terms in the chapter to solve the puzzle. Most clues come from the chapter text, some require outside investigation. Omit spaces or dashes between words.

Solution:

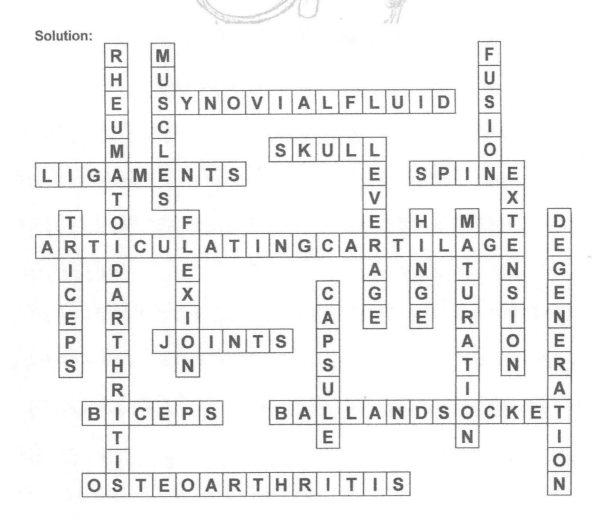

Fever and Cough

Vocabulary 1: Definitions

Directions: Use the text, a dictionary, or the internet to write a definition for each term.

1. viral infection: **infection caused by a virus, such as influenza or zika**

2. mononucleosis: **known as kissing disease, a viral illness spread in saliva**

3. measles: **infectious childhood viral disease causing skin rash**

4. chicken pox: **childhood viral illness that can reappear years later as shingles**

5. lymph nodes: **small bodies along lymphatic system that filter bacteria as part of our immune system**

6. thyroid gland: **gland in neck producing hormones affecting metabolic rate**

7. rhonchi: **rattling, low pitch sounds emanating from the lungs**

8. sputum: **a mixture of saliva and mucous from the respiratory tract**

9. bowel sounds: **normal sounds from abdomen caused by peristalsis**

10. genetic disease: **a disorder caused by abnormal gene(s) inherited from one or both parents**

11. infectious disease: **illness caused by bacteria, viruses, fungi, or parasites**

12. malignancy: **the presence of cancer**

Investigation 3.8A

Fever and Cough

Vocabulary 2: Matching

Directions: Match the definitions on the right to the medical terms on the left.

1. __D__ viral infection

2. __K__ mononucleosis

3. __H__ measles

4. __B__ chicken pox

5. __E__ lymph nodes

6. __L__ thyroid gland

7. __G__ rhonchi

8. __A__ sputum

9. __I__ bowel sounds

10. __F__ genetic disease

11. __C__ infectious disease

12. __J__ malignancy

a. a mixture of saliva and mucous from the respiratory tract

b. children viral illness that can reappear years later as shingles

c. illness caused by bacteria, viruses, fungi, or parasites

d. infection caused by a virus, such as influenza or zika

e. small bodies along lymphatic system that filter bacteria as part of our immune system

f. a disorder caused by abnormal gene(s) inherited from one or both parents

g. rattling, low pitch sounds emanating from the lungs

h. infectious childhood viral disease causing skin rash

i. normal sounds from abdomen caused by peristalsis

j. the presence of cancer

k. known as kissing disease, a viral illness spread in saliva

l. gland in neck producing hormones affecting metabolic rate

Investigation 3.8A

Fever and Cough

Vocabulary 3: Sentences

Dr. _____

P._____Date_____

Directions: Use each term in a complete sentence.

1. viral infection: _____
    _____

2. mononucleosis:_____
    _____

3. measles: _____
    _____

4. chicken pox: _____
    _____

5. lymph nodes: _____
    _____

6. thyroid gland: _____
    _____

7. rhonchi: _____
    _____

8. sputum: _____
    _____

9. bowel sounds: _____
    _____

10. genetic disease: _____
    _____

11. infectious disease: _____
    _____

12. malignancy: _____
    _____

Worksheet : Fever & Cough

Fever & Cough

Patient Name: **Manjula Mehroul**   Age: **20**   Gender: **female**

Wt: **127** lbs.   Respirations: **18** /min   Pulse: **86** /min

Blood Pressure: **122 /76** mmHg   Temperature: **98.8° F**.

CC: **fever and cough 4 weeks duration**

HxCC: (List important information from the patient in your history of the chief complaint)

1. **visited India 2 months ago for one week**

2. **patient feels major fatigue**

3. **recurrent fever**

4. **day & night violent cough attacks**

5. **thick mucus with blood**

6. **non-smoker**

7. **grandmother died after unknown illness**

8. **negative for sore throat, tonsils, sinuses, lymph glands**

ROS: (List all positive findings from Review of Systems)-

1. **measles & chicken pox in childhood**

2. **had usual childhood immunizations**

3. **negative surgical history**

4. **negative hospitalizations**

5. **negative for rash or painful lymph nodes**

Positive Examination Findings:

1. **pulse 86/ min, temperature 98.8**

2. **Rhonchi left lung**

3. **mucus collected**

4. **no palpable nodes**

DDX: (List your three most likely diagnoses from the Diagnosis Grid)

1. **mononucleosis**

2. **tuberculosis**

3. **pneumonia**

DDX-2: List the disorders from your DDX list you **ruled out** immediately because their symptoms did not fit this patient's history and physical exam findings:

1. **Hodgkins Lymphoma**

2. **Lung Cancer**

3. **non-Hodgkins Lymphoma**

Put an X next to the tests you select first to investigate this patient's medical problem. Write <u>NA</u> for any test listed that is probably not appropriate to your evaluation of this condition:

- __X__   X-rays of chest and lungs

- __X__   Complete Blood Count (CBC)

- _____   MRI of the Chest

- _____   Ultrasound Study of chest

- __X__   Culture and Sensitivity of Sputum

- _+ -_   PPD test for TB

Lab Test Results:

• Lab Test	• Normal	• Results
• Chest X-Ray	• Lungs clear • Immediate results	• Positive for cavities in left lung
• PPD	• Results in 3 days • No reaction	• Positive reaction • Redness at test site
• Culture & Sensitivity of Sputum	• Light diverse bacterial growth	• Acid-Fast Bacilli smear and culture positive for (TB) Mycobacterium tuberculosis

Lab Test Summary: Record positive lab test findings from your lab tests (above):

1. **Chest X-ray positive for cavities in left lung**

2. **Sputum Culture & Sensitivity positive for Acid-Fast Bacilli/Mycobacterium Tuberculosis**

3. **PPD positive reaction after 3 days**

How do we know the lung cavities seen on the chest x-ray are in the left lung?

The left lung has two lobes, while the right lung has three lobes.

Why was it important to take a Chest x-ray instead of waiting for the PPD test or the sputum culture?

It is important to take a chest x-ray because the results are immediate. You then have evidence the patient should not be in the public domain, exposing others to her illness. Measures can be taken to prevent spreading of the bacteria.

Your Diagnosis? (Hint: It is listed on the DDX list)

Tuberculosis

Treatment Recommendations (Select type of treatment(s) you would recommend)

    a. **begin antibiotic treatment based on culture and sensitivity results**

    b. **patient encouraged to stay away from the public**

    c. **patient wear a surgical mask to keep bacteria isolated**

Check the appropriate box to indicate how <u>Tuberculosis</u> spreads from one person to another (more than one method of spreading may exist):

TB Method of spreading	yes	no
• Breathing TB droplets in the air	x	
• Skin to skin contact with another person		x
• Touching contaminated door handle		x
• Sharing a glass		x
• Contact with contaminated blood		x
• Kissing a TB infected person		x
• Contact with bedding or toilet seat		x
• Cannot be spread to others		x

Why do you think antibiotics have worked in the past to cure tuberculosis, but more recently may not work so well?

Bacteria are constantly changing due to their rapid reproductive cycle and mutations occurring in the genetic make-up. Over time the mutations accommodate for the antibiotics they have been exposed to and make them resistant.

Reflections:

1. What was your patient's chief complaint? **fever and cough, duration 4 weeks**

2. Would you consider Manjula's complaint to be:

   (circle)   Acute   **<u>Subacute</u>**   or   Chronic

   a. Why?

   Her symptoms have been ongoing for the past four weeks

166

3. How would you classify Manjula's condition (circle your answer)?

                    Possible Emergency   or   Probably Non-Emergency

4. Why is Manjula's condition an **emergency** or non-emergency?

    The emergency does not pertain to impending immediate death to Manjula, but rather that allowing her back into the public can rapidly spread the disease to others.

5. Which DDx possibilities did you **rule out** right away?

    a. **Hodgkins Lymphoma**

    b. **Lung Cancer**

    c. **non-Hodgkins Lymphoma**

6. Is Tuberculosis caused by an injury or __illness__? (Circle your answer)

7. Is Tuberculosis preventable? How or why not?
    Tuberculosis __is preventable__ because there is now a vaccine available. However, the vaccine is not generally made available the United States due to the low incidence of tuberculosis in our population.

8. Why is it important to diagnose and treat patients suspected of having Tuberculosis?
    It is important to diagnose and treat tuberculosis because it is highly contagious through coughing as an airborne spread illness. Tuberculosis kills millions of people around the world each year.

Crossword   **Fever & Cough**

Directions: Use the highlighted terms in the chapter to solve the puzzle. Most clues come from the chapter text, some require outside investigation. Omit spaces or dashes between words.

Solution:

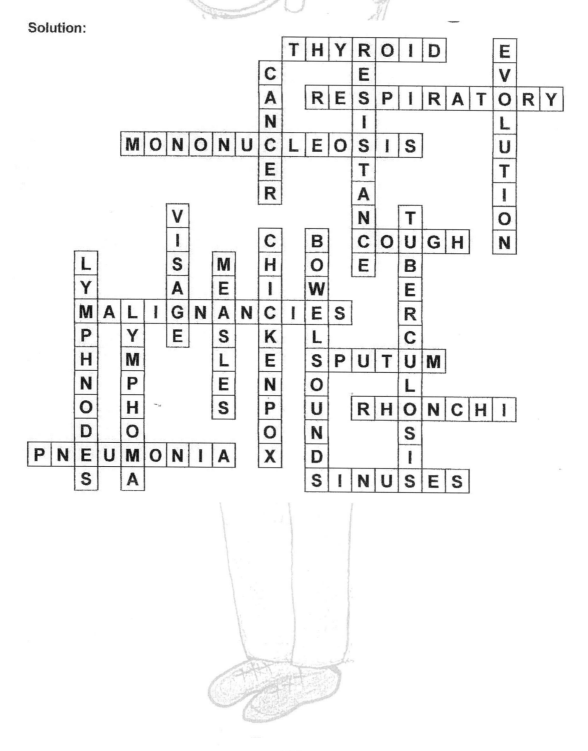

Pulmonary Embolism

Vocabulary 1: Definitions

Directions: Use the text, a dictionary, or the internet to write a definition for each term.

1. respiratory system: __the group of organs that allows us to breathe and exchange__
    __oxygen and carbon dioxide throughout the body__

2. carbon dioxide: __removed from the atmosphere by plants, exhaled by humans__

3. oxygen: __inhaled by humans, given off by plants__

4. diaphragm: __dome-shaped muscle that contracts for inspiration and relaxes during__
    __exhalation__

5. trachea: __the windpipe; tube through which air moves to and from the lungs__

6. epiglottis: __cartilaginous cover that keeps food out of our windpipe__

7. emphysema: __disorder where the lungs air sacs are damaged, common in smokers__

8. carcinogenic: __anything thought to have the potential to cause cancer__

9. bronchi: __the two main branches of the trachea heading toward the lung__

10. villi: __hair-like structures in our respiratory tract that helps move mucous upward__

11. bronchioles: __the many tiny air tubes connecting the bronchi to the alveoli__

12. alveoli: __the respiratory system air sacs where oxygen/carbon dioxide exchange occurs__

Vocabulary 2: Matching

Directions: Match the definitions on the right to the medical terms on the left.

1. __E__ respiratory system

2. __H__ carbon dioxide

3. __B__ oxygen

4. __G__ diaphragm

5. __J__ trachea

6. __C__ epiglottis

7. __F__ emphysema

8. __K__ carcinogenic

9. __I__ bronchi

10. __D__ villi

11. __L__ bronchioles

12. __A__ alveoli

a. The respiratory system air sacs where oxygen/carbon dioxide exchange occurs

b. Inhaled by humans, given off by plants

c. cartilaginous cover that keeps food out of our windpipe

d. hair-like structures in our respiratory tract that helps move mucous upward

e. the group of organs that allows us to breathe and exchange oxygen and carbon dioxide throughout the body

f. disorder where the lungs air sacs are damaged, common in smokers

g. dome-shaped muscle that contracts for inspiration and relaxes during exhalation

h. removed from the atmosphere by plants, exhaled by humans

i. the two main branches of the trachea heading toward the lungs

j. the windpipe; tube through which air moves to and from the lungs

k. anything thought to have the potential to cause cancer

l. the many tiny air tubes connecting the bronchi to the alveoli

Dr. _____

P._____Date_____

Vocabulary 3: Sentences

Directions: Use each term in a complete sentence.

1. respiratory system: _____
   _____

2. carbon dioxide: _____
   _____

3. oxygen: _____
   _____

4. diaphragm: _____
   _____

5. trachea: _____
   _____

6. epiglottis: _____
   _____

7. emphysema: _____
   _____

8. carcinogenic: _____
   _____

9. bronchi: _____
   _____

10. villi: _____
    _____

11. bronchioles: _____
    _____

12. alveoli: _____
    _____

Investigation 3.8B: Respiratory System

Worksheet 3.8

Directions: Answer the questions based on your reading of 3.8B.

1. Air enters the respiratory system by way of the **nose** and **mouth**.

2. The two main ingredients in our air are **oxygen** and **nitrogen**.

3. **Nitrogen** (a gas) makes up 78% of the air we breathe.

4. The **epiglottis** covers the trachea and protects the airway from food and liquids from the mouth.

5. The lungs are located in the **thorax (chest)**.

6. Air travels to the lungs by moving through the **respiratory** system.

7. Air enters the lungs by way of the **bronchi**.

8. From the bronchi the air then moves to the **bronchioles**.

9. Oxygen is exchanged for carbon dioxide in the **alveoli**.

10. The lining covering the lungs is the **pleura**.

11. What provides the energy for inspiration (breathing in)?

      intercostal muscles

      diaphragm

12. What happens to allow us to exhale air from our lungs?

      a. **relaxation of the diaphragm**

      b. **elasticity of the lungs**

13. Name three ways we might expose our lungs to a toxic environment.

      a. **smoking (inhaling hot air and chemicals)**

      b. **2nd hand smoke (toxic chemicals)**

      c. **breathing in disease-causing microbes, pollens, and airborne chemicals**

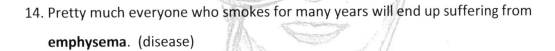

14. Pretty much everyone who smokes for many years will end up suffering from

    emphysema. (disease)

15. What names have been given to those suffering from emphysema?

    pink puffers and blue blotters

16. Many people who smoke for many years end up with what diseases?

    emphysema

    lung cancer

17. Tar in cigarettes is considered a **carcinogen**, which means it can cause cancer.

18. Children exposed to second hand smoke and other air-toxins can develop

    asthma.

19. Which area of the lung is most destroyed by smoking?   **alveoli**

20. What function do villi perform in our trachea?

    Villi are responsible to move mucus up and out of the trachea.

Worksheet 3.8.B, page 3

Directions: Write the names of the structures of the respiratory tract next to the number.

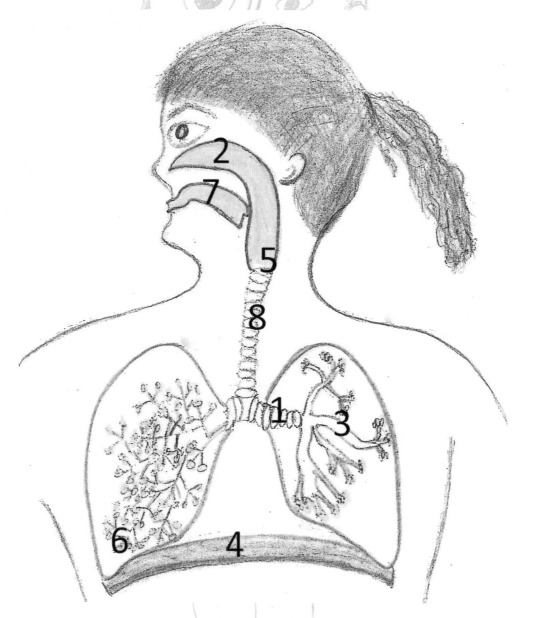

1. __**BRONCHI**__

2. __**NASAL PASSAGE**__

3. __**BRONCHIOLE**__

4. __**DIAPHRAGM**__

5. __**EPIGLOTTIS**__

6. __**ALVEOLI**__

7. __**MOUTH**__

8. __**TRACHEA**__

Crossword   **Lungs**

Directions: Use the highlighted terms in the chapter to solve the puzzle. Most clues come from the chapter text, some require outside investigation. Omit spaces or dashes between words.

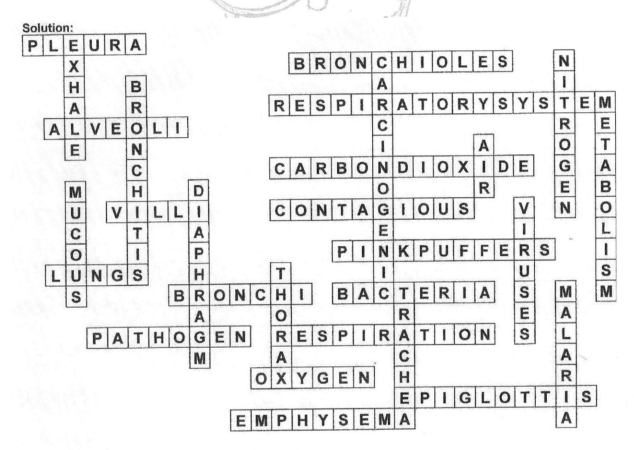

Solution:

Abdominal Pain & Dark Urine

Vocabulary 1: Definitions

Directions: Use the text, a dictionary, or the internet to write a definition for each term.

1. general anesthesia: __inducing a state of unconsciousness with the absence of pain perception over the entire body__

2. consultation: __a physician having special training examines another physician's patient__

3. immunizations: __vaccinations that provide immunity to bacterial or viral diseases__

4. hypertension: __an ongoing condition of elevated blood pressure__

5. hematuria: __the presence of blood in the urine; blood in the urine is always abnormal__

6. blood urea nitrogen: __test measuring the amount of nitrogen in the blood performed to determine how well the kidneys are functioning__

7. creatinine: __a waste product of muscle metabolism filtered out by kidneys and eliminated in urine__

8. kidney filtration rate: __the flow rate of filtered fluid through the kidneys__

9. intravenous pyelogram: __an x-ray examination of the kidneys, ureters, and urinary bladder using injected iodinated contrast material__

10. bedside manner: __the doctor's approach or attitude towards his/her patients__

11. autosomal dominant: __passing on a trait or disorder where the gene is expressed, even if carried by only one parent__

12. polycystic kidney disease: __a genetic disorder where abnormal cysts form and grow in the kidneys__

Abdominal Pain & Dark Urine

Vocabulary 2: Matching

Directions: Match the definitions on the right to the medical terms on the left.

b. an ongoing condition of elevated blood pressure

1. __I__ general anesthesia

c. test measuring the amount of nitrogen in the blood performed to determine how well the kidneys are functioning

2. __A__ consultation

3. __H__ immunizations

d. the flow rate of filtered fluid through the kidneys

4. __B__ hypertension

e. the doctor's approach or attitude towards his/her patients

5. __L__ hematuria

f. a genetic disorder where abnormal cysts form and grow in the kidneys

6. __C__ blood urea nitrogen

7. __K__ creatinine

g. an x-ray examination of the kidneys, ureters, and urinary bladder using injected iodinated contrast material

8. __D__ kidney filtration rate

9. __G__ intravenous pyelogram

h. vaccinations that provide immunity to bacterial or viral diseases

10. __E__ bedside manner

i. inducing a state of unconsciousness with the absence of pain perception over the entire body

11. __J__ autosomal dominant

j. passing on a trait or disorder where the gene is expressed, even if carried by only one parent

12. __F__ polycystic kidney disease

k. a waste product of muscle metabolism filtered out by kidneys and eliminated in urine

a. a physician having special training examines another physician's patient

l. the presence of blood in the urine; blood in the urine is always abnormal

Investigation 3.9A

Abdominal Pain & Dark Urine

Vocabulary 3: Sentences

Dr. _____

P._____Date_____

Directions: Write a sentence using each term.

1. general anesthesia: _____

_____

2. consultation:_____

_____

3. immunizations: _____

_____

4. hypertension: _____

_____

5. hematuria: _____

_____

6. blood urea nitrogen: _____

_____

7. creatinine: _____

_____

8. kidney filtration rate: _____

_____

9. intravenous pyelogram: _____

_____

10. bedside manner: _____

_____

11. autosomal dominant: _____

_____

12. polycystic kidney disease: _____

_____

Worksheet 3.9A: Abdominal and Back Pain and Dark Urine

Directions: Answer the following questions which are based on your reading of the preceding case study.

1. As the consulting physician in this case, which specialty of medicine do you most likely practice? **nephrologist or urologist**

2. What may be America's greatest contribution to healthcare?

     general anesthesia

3. As the consulting physician on a patient you do not know, what is the first step in beginning to understand the reason you are examining the patient?

   examine the patient's hospital chart

4. What medical issues are documented in the history and physical from Dr. Johnson?
   a. **steady trend toward hypertension (high blood pressure)**
   b. **hematuria (blood in urine)**
   c. **abdominal or flank pain**
   d. **loss of appetite**

5. What medication does Martha take each day? **Lisinopril 10 mg q.d. (once a day)**

6. What lab test result gave you a great deal of information?

     kidney filtration rate

7. What is the normal kidney filtration rate**?   > 90 mL/min**

8. What was Martha's kidney filtration rate?   **64 mL/min**

9. What are the two positive findings in your examination?

     hematuria (blood in the urine)

     elevated blood pressure (148/94 mm Hg)

Investigation 3.9A – Abdominal and Back Pain and Dark Urine

Worksheet, Page 2   Teacher

Disease	Nausea/ Vomit	Pain	Pain	Painful Urination	Fever/ Chills	Hematuria	Frequent Urination	Other
Urinary Infection	X	Upper back	side	X	X	X	X	acute
Pyelo-nephritis	X	Upper back	side	X	X		X	Acute or chronic
Kidney Stones	X	Sudden, severe abdominal				X		acute
Upper Urinary Tract Infection	X		side	X	X		X	acute
Cystitis		pelvic		X	X	X	X	Acute or chronic
Kidney Cancer		Low back or none	mass		X	X		Appetite loss
Polycystic Kidney Disease		abdominal	side	If kidney stones		X	X	Hyper-tension chronic
Leptso-spirosis	X	Headache, low back,	calf		X			Jaundice, appetite loss
Martha		**ABD**			**slight**	**X**	**X**	**Appetite loss**

Add Martha's symptoms at the **bottom row** of the chart and compare them to the rest of the differential diagnosis list.

Worksheet 3.9, page 3

10. Which disease(s) do Martha's symptoms most match?

   Polycystic Kidney Disease

11. What is hematuria?   **blood in the urine**

12. What is the purpose of Lisinopril? **Treatment of hypertension (increased blood pressure)**

13. What potential problem can a IVP (intravenous pyelogram) cause that makes you hesitant to utilize this test? **the contrast material can damage the kidney and make Martha's condition worse.**

14. What test did you order to evaluate Martha's kidneys?   **ultrasound**

15. What were the findings of the test ordered in #14?

   kidney cysts, 3 right & 2 left kidney

16. What do the test results confirm as your diagnosis?

   Autosomal Dominant Polycystic Kidney Disease

17. Is this disease infectious or genetic?   **genetic**

18. Is this disease acute or chronic? **chronic**

19. What are the 3 important functions of the kidneys?

   a. **filter waste products from blood**

   b. **maintain blood pressure**

   c. **produce urine**

20. Why would Martha take a blood pressure medicine when she has kidney disease?

   to try to control her blood pressure

21. Is Polycystic Kidney Disease a local disease or diffuse? **diffuse**

22. What other complications can occur in this disease?

   abnormal blood vessels in the brain

   leaking heart valves

   recurrent urinary tract infections

23. Why would it be important to advise Martha's children's pediatrician of her condition?

Autosomal Dominant Polycystic Kidney disease is a genetic disorder having a 50% chance of passing on to each offspring.

24. Is there a cure for Martha's illness?   **No**

25. Could Martha ever be a candidate for a kidney transplant?   **Yes**

26. Do you think it would be difficult to tell Martha about her illness? Why?

It would be difficult to tell Martha about her illness because:

    a.   it is an incurable genetic disorder

    b.   it has a 50% chance of being passed on to each of her offspring.

Crossword   **Abdominal Pain**

Directions: Use the highlighted terms in the chapter to solve the puzzle. Most clues come from the chapter text, but some require outside investigation. Omit spaces or dashes between words.

Solution:

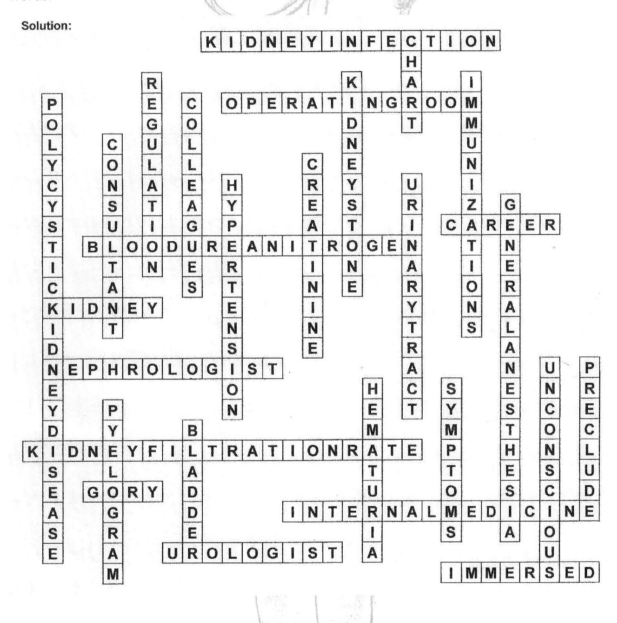

Urinary Tract

Vocabulary 1: Definitions

Directions: Use the text, a dictionary, or the internet to write a definition for each term.

1. urinary tract: **the system of organs that filter waste from blood and produce, store, and discharge urine**

2. kidneys: **the organs that filter waste from blood and produce urine**

3. hormone: **chemical produced in a gland that controls the function of other glands or organs**

4. renal: **relating to the kidneys**

5. nephrons: **the part of the kidney where waste products are filtered from blood and urine produced**

6. sphincter: **the ring of muscle that prevents constant flow of urine**

7. micturition reflex: **the signal telling you it's time to pee; occurs in response to increased bladder pressure**

8. sterile: **the absence of bacteria and other living microorganisms**

9. urinary bladder: **the hollow organ that collects and stores urine until it exits through the urethra**

10. urethra: **the duct that carries urine from the urinary bladder to the outside world**

11. ureter: **tube that sends urine from the kidneys to the urinary bladder**

12. urinary catheter: **a tube inserted through the urethra into the urinary bladder to allow urine to drain**

Investigation 3.9B

Urinary Tract

Vocabulary 2: Matching

Directions: Match the definitions on the right to the medical terms on the left.

1. __B__ urinary tract

2. __F__ kidneys

3. __J__ hormone

4. __C__ renal

5. __A__ nephrons

6. __G__ sphincter

7. __L__ micturition reflex

8. __E__ sterile

9. __I__ urinary bladder

10. __D__ urethra

11. __K__ ureter

12. __H__ urinary catheter

a. The part of the kidney where waste products are filtered from blood and urine produced

b. the system of organs that filter waste from blood and produce, store, and discharge urine

c. relating to the kidneys

d. the duct that carries urine from the urinary bladder to the outside world

e. the absence of bacteria and other living microorganisms

f. the organs that filter waste from blood and produce urine

g. the ring of muscle that prevents constant flow of urine

h. a tube inserted through the urethra into the urinary bladder to allow urine to drain

i. the hollow organ that collects and stores urine until it exits through the urethra

j. chemical produced in a gland that controls the function of other glands or organs

k. tube that sends urine from the kidneys to the urinary bladder

l. the signal telling you it's time to pee; occurs in response to increased bladder pressure

Urinary Tract

Vocabulary 3: Sentences

Directions: Use each term in a sentence.

1. urinary tract: _____

   _____

2. kidneys:_____

   _____

3. hormone: _____

   _____

4. renal: _____

   _____

5. nephrons: _____

   _____

6. sphincter: _____

   _____

7. micturition reflex: _____

   _____

8. sterile: _____

   _____

9. urinary bladder:_____

   _____

10. urethra:_____

    _____

11. ureter:_____

    _____

12. urinary catheter:_____

    _____

Worksheet 3.9B: Urinary Tract

1. What are the four main parts of the urinary tract?

    a. **kidneys**

    b. **ureters**

    c. **urinary bladder**

    d. **urethra**

2. What does 'renal' refer to?   **kidneys**

3. How many kidneys do normal babies have at birth?   **two**

4. How does blood enter and leave the kidneys?

    Enters: **Renal Arteries**

    Departs: **Renal Veins**

5. What percent of material that filters through the kidneys returns to the blood?

    99 %

6. What do we call the little tubes inside the kidneys that do the complex filtering process?

    nephrons

7. About how many quarts of filtrate pass through the tubules of the kidneys per day?

    150   quarts/day

8. Approximately how much urine is produced every day?   **1 – 2   quarts/day**

9. How much water do doctors recommend we drink each day to keep our kidneys filtering

    efficiently?   **6 – 8   glasses**

10. Through what structure must urine travel to get from the kidney to the bladder?

    Ureter

11. What causes urine to move from the kidneys to the bladder?

    a. **gravity**

    b. **smooth muscle**

12. What is the purpose of the bladder?

    storage of urine until the opportunity arises to go pee

13. Which reflex lets us know that it is time to urinate?

    micturition reflex

14. What acts as a facet to start and stop the flow of urine?

    a sphincter

15. How does urine get from the bladder to the outside world?

    via the **urethra**

16. Is urine sterile?   YES   **NO**   (circle your answer)

17. What is the main ingredient in urine? 95% **water**

18. Why do you think there is so much nitrogen present in urine?

Nitrogen's presence in urine comes from the stomach breaking down proteins.

Urinary Tract Worksheet – Diagram

Worksheet 3.9B

Directions: Identify the parts of the urinary system and write their names on the line of the corresponding number.

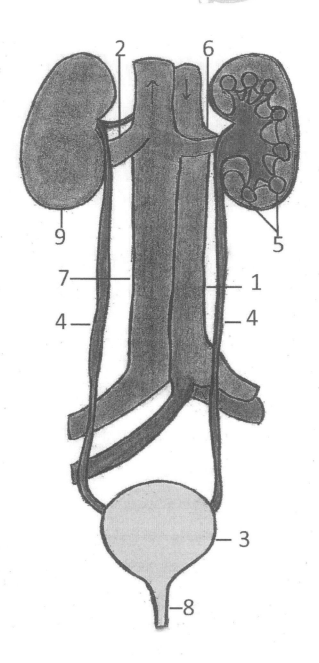

Urinary Tract

1. ABDOMINAL AORTA

2. RENAL VEIN

3. URINARY BLADDER

4. URETER

5. NEPHRONS

6. RENAL ARTERY

7. INFERIOR VENA CAVA

8. URETHRA

9. KIDNEY

Investigation 3.9B

Crossword 3.9B   **Urinary Tract**

Directions: Use the highlighted terms in the chapter to solve the puzzle. Most clues come from the chapter text, some require outside investigation. Omit spaces or dashes between words.

Solution:

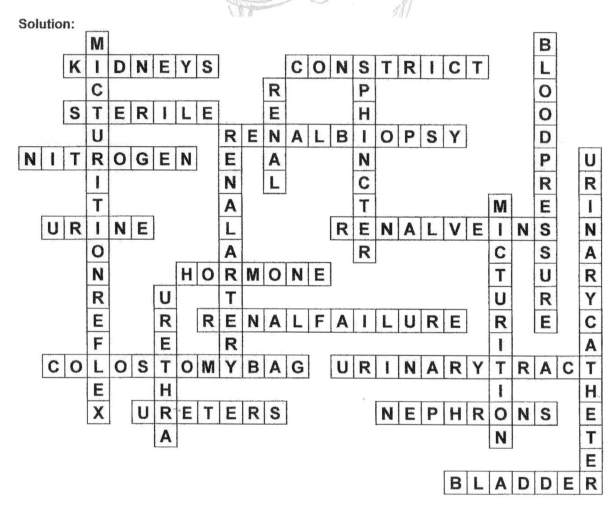

Weak & Dizzy

Vocabulary 1: Definitions

Directions: Use the text, a dictionary, or the internet to write a definition for each term.

1. lymph nodes: _small bodies along lymphatic system that filter bacteria_

2. palpation: _using the hands to examine the body while diagnosing illness_

3. liver: _large, glandular organ located in right upper quadrant, makes bile and involved in many metabolic processes_

4. hyperpigmentation: _darkening of an area of skin or nails caused by increased melanin_

5. estrogen: _hormones that promote the development of female characteristics_

6. pneumonia: _lung inflammation caused by bacterial or viral infection_

7. shingles: _acute inflammation along a nerve with skin rash caused by recurrence of chicken pox virus_

8. tetanus booster: _vaccine given during childhood and then every ten years thereafter to stimulate immunity to tetanus_

9. Mees' lines: _horizontal white lines across finger and toenails representing exposure to arsenic_

10. arsenic: _element #33, a poison commonly found in insecticides and rat poisons, causes Mee's lines_

11. metabolize: _breaking down food into a form usable by your body_

12. excreted: _discharged or given off as waste matter, such as carbon dioxide, urine, sweat, & feces_

Weak and Dizzy

Vocabulary 2: Matching

Directions: Match the definitions on the right to the medical terms on the left.

1. __F__ lymph nodes

2. __B__ palpation

3. __A__ liver

4. __J__ hyperpigmentation

5. __E__ estrogen

6. __K__ pneumonia

7. __I__ shingles

8. __D__ tetanus booster

9. __H__ Mee's lines

10. __L__ arsenic

11. __C__ metabolize

12. __G__ excreted

a. Large, glandular organ located in left upper quadrant, makes bile and involved in many metabolic processes

b. using the hands to examine the body while diagnosing illness

c. breaking down food into a form usable by your body

d. vaccine given during childhood and then every ten years thereafter to stimulate immunity to tetanus

e. hormones that promote the development of female characteristics

f. small bodies along lymphatic system that filter bacteria

g. discharged or given off as waste matter, such as carbon dioxide, urine, sweat, & feces

h. horizontal white lines across finger and toenails representing exposure to arsenic

i. acute inflammation along a nerve with skin rash caused by recurrence of chicken pox virus

j. darkening of an area of skin or nails caused by increased melanin

k. lung inflammation caused by bacterial or viral infection

l. element #33, a poison commonly found in insecticides and rat poisons, causes Mee's lines

Investigation 3.10A

Weak & Dizzy

Vocabulary 3: Sentences

Dr. _____

P._____ Date_____

Directions: Use each term in a sentence.

1. lymph nodes: _____

    _____

2. palpation: _____

    _____

3. liver: _____

    _____

4. hyperpigmentation: _____

    _____

5. estrogen: _____

    _____

6. pneumonia: _____

    _____

7. shingles: _____

    _____

8. tetanus booster: _____

    _____

9. Mees' lines: _____

    _____

10. arsenic: _____

    _____

11. metabolize: _____

    _____

12. excreted: _____

    _____

Investigation 3.10A: Weak & Dizzy
Worksheet 3.10A

Directions: Refer to Investigation 3.10A to answer the following questions.

1. List Dorothy's symptoms that something is affecting her health:

   a. **feels weak**

   b. **dizzy**

   c. **unstable on feet**

   d. **aching in hands and feet**

   e. **lack of appetite**

   f. **stomach discomfort/diarrhea**

2. What objective findings did you see in her physical examination?

   a. **sick appearance**

   b. **listless**

   c. **disengaged**

   d. **abdominal tenderness of palpation**

   e. **dry skin**

   f. **slight swelling of feet and ankles**

   g. **scattered areas of hyperpigmentation**

3. Which laboratory tests did you order on Dorothy's first visit?

   a. **Complete Blood Count (CBC)**

   b. **Electrolytes and Blood Urea Nitrogen (BUN) (kidney blood test)**

   c. **Complete Blood Metabolic Panel (liver blood test)**

   d. **Cardiac Enzymes (heart blood test)**

   e. **Urinalysis**

4. What new symptoms did you observe at the second meeting with this patient?

   a. **Conjunctival Icterus (yellowing of eye sclera)**

   b. **enlarged, tender liver**

   c. **Mee's lines in finger nails**

5. What is the significance of Mee's Lines?

   Mee's lines appear in cases of arsenic poisoning

6. Which parts of the body are primarily affected in arsenic toxicity?

   a. **skin**

   b. **lungs**

   c. **bladder**

   d. **liver**

   e. **kidneys**

7. Where in the body is arsenic deposited that can easily be utilized to make a definitive diagnosis of arsenic toxicity?

   nails and hair

8. What signs did Dorothy demonstrate that could indicate early pulmonary damage?

   rapid respiratory rate (24 breaths/min)

9. How can chronic arsenic exposure cause bladder cancer

   Bladder tissue is very sensitive to toxins. Arsenic expelled in urine sits for hours in bladder until urination occurs.

10. What potential danger exists from buying fruits and vegetables imported from other countries?

    Fruits and vegetables may have been grown in arsenic contaminated soil or watered with arsenic contaminated water.

11. Which medical laboratory test from the earlier list would you order to confirm your diagnosis of heavy metal poisoning with arsenic?

    Heavy Metals Panel (blood test)

Investigation 3.10A

Teacher

Crossword 3.10A **Weak & Dizzy**

Directions: Use the highlighted terms in the chapter to solve the puzzle. Most clues come from the chapter text, some require outside investigation. Omit spaces or dashes between words.

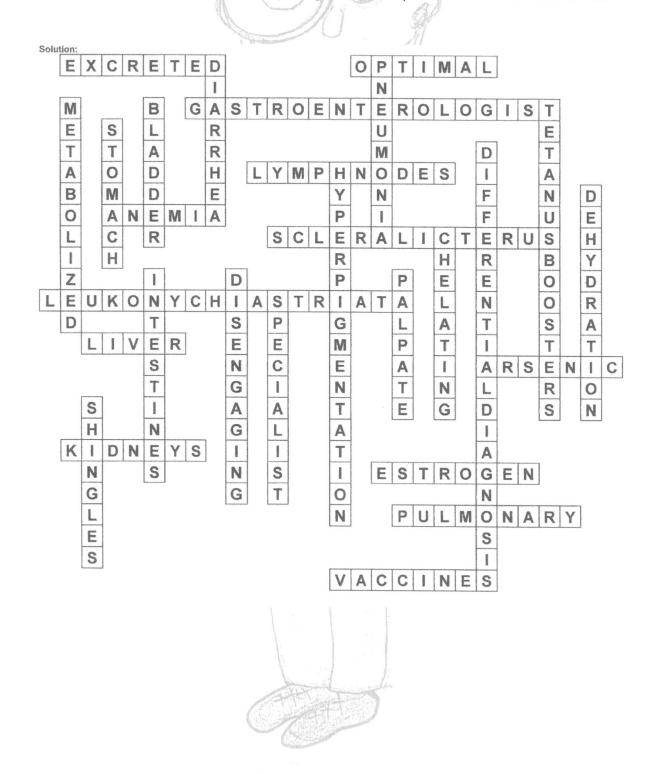

Solution:

EXCRETED   OPTIMAL

GASTROENTEROLOGIST

LYMPHNODES

ANEMIA

SCLERALICTERUS

LEUKONYCHIASTRIATA

LIVER

ARSENIC

KIDNEYS

ESTROGEN

PULMONARY

VACCINES

Environmental Toxins

Vocabulary 1: Definitions

Directions: Use the text, a dictionary, or the internet to write a definition for each term.

1. toxins: __poisonous substances capable of causing health problems__

2. debilitating: __a disease or condition that makes someone very weak and unhealthy__

3. lead: __atomic number 82, Pb has been used in water carrying pipes, especially toxic to children__

4. cadmium: __metal used in chrome rims and rechargeable batteries, toxic to humans__

5. mercury: __element #80, a toxic metal used at one time in thermometers, batteries, florescent lights, and more__

6. radioactive: __having or producing powerful and dangerous radiation; overexposure linked to cancer__

7. PCB's: __toxic compounds used in the manufacture of plastics__

8. pesticides: __chemicals used to kill pests that also get into our water and land__

9. prescription drugs: __chemicals prescribed by physicians affecting the human body in negative ways when misused__

10. World Health Organization: __agency of the United Nations concerned with international public health__

11. carcinogenic: __potentially capable of causing cancer__

12. chronic exposure: __repeated contact over a protracted period of time__

Environmental Toxins

Vocabulary 2: Matching

Directions: Match the definitions on the right to the terms on the left.

1. __L__ toxins

2. __E__ debilitating

3. __K__ lead

4. __C__ cadmium

5. __I__ mercury

6. __J__ radioactive

7. __F__ PCB's

8. __A__ pesticides

9. __H__ prescription drugs

10. __D__ World Health Organization

11. __G__ carcinogenic

12. __B__ chronic exposure

a. chemicals used to kill pests that also get into our water and land

b. repeated contact over a protracted period of time

c. metal used in chrome rims and rechargeable batteries, toxic to humans

d. agency of the United Nations concerned with international public health

e. a disease or condition that makes someone very weak and unhealthy

f. toxic compounds used in the manufacture of plastics

g. potentially capable of causing cancer

h. chemicals prescribed by physicians affecting the human body in negative ways when misused

i. element #80, a toxic metal used at one time in thermometers, batteries, florescent lights, and more

j. having or producing powerful and dangerous radiation; overexposure linked to cancer

k. atomic number 82, Pb has been used in water carrying pipes, especially toxic to children

l. poisonous substances capable of causing health problems

Investigation 3.10B

Environmental Toxins

Vocabulary 3: Sentences

Dr. _____

P._____Date_____

Directions: Use each term in a sentence.

1. toxins: _____
   _____

2. debilitating:_____
   _____

3. lead: _____
   _____

4. cadmium: _____
   _____

5. mercury: _____
   _____

6. radioactive: _____
   _____

7. PCB's: _____
   _____

8. pesticides: _____
   _____

9. prescription drugs: _____
   _____

10. World Health Organization: _____
    _____

11. carcinogenic: _____
    _____

12. chronic exposure: _____
    _____

Environmental Toxins

Directions: Answer the following questions based on your reading of investigation 3.10B, Environmental Toxins.

1. What international organization tracks environmental toxins around the world?

    Pure Earth

2. Potential sources of environmental toxins, even here in the U.S., can be found in:

    a. **lead**   (any five)

    b. **cadmium**

    c. **mercury**

    d. **radon & uranium**

    e. **pesticides & plastics**

3. Which toxin does Pure Earth continue to rate as the leading debilitating toxin in the entire world?

    lead

4. Which heavy metal toxin, also associated with the processing of car batteries, has poisoned U.S. citizens' water supply and was once found in paint?

    lead

5. Which heavy metal affected first responders to the World Trade Center terrorist attack?

    cadmium

6. Formerly used in thermometers, construction, florescent lights, and many other things, this heavy metal has spread into our lakes and oceans and into our fish supply, including tuna, swordfish, shark and King mackerel. This heavy metal is: **mercury**

7. Our government's testing of nuclear materials and building of nuclear power plants has exposed our citizens to the potential of poisoning by which heavy metal?

    uranium

8. Which two countries experienced very serious nuclear disasters related to the operation of their nuclear power plants?

   a. Russia

   b. Japan

9. Which pesticide was used extensively to control mosquitos and pests attacked crops until 1972, yet still contaminates our air, water, and soil?

   DDT

10. What have the burning fossil fuels in our cars, trucks, trains, planes, and factories worldwide spewed into our air that scientists feel has raised the CO2 level of our atmosphere and caused climate change?

    a. Carbon Monoxide

    b. Carbon Dioxide

11. About how many people does the World Health Organization estimate die each year as a direct result of air pollution?

    4.6 million people each year

12. Why does most exposure to toxic chemicals occur inside the home?
    Most people spend 90% of their time indoors, bombarded by fumes given off by carpets, stoves, heaters, fireplaces, and more. Many are exposed to cigarette smoke as well.

13. Write a paragraph explaining your thoughts about the greatest environmental concerns for the area where you live.

    _____

    _____

    _____

    _____

    _____

    _____

    _____

Crossword 3.10B   **Environmental Toxins**

Directions: Use the highlighted terms in the chapter to solve the puzzle. Most clues come from the chapter text, but some require outside investigation. Omit spaces or dashes between words.

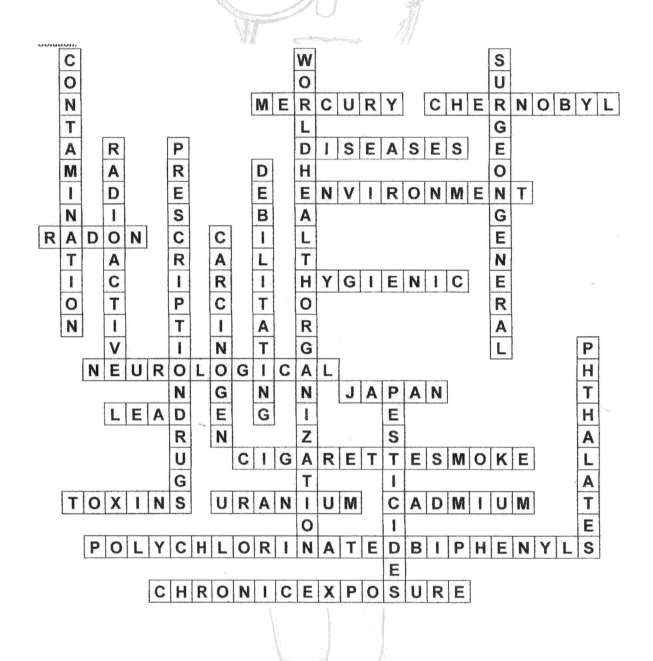

Food-borne Illness

Vocabulary 1: Definitions

Directions: Use the text, a dictionary, or the internet to write a definition for each term.

1. Food-borne illness: **food poisoning; illness resulting from eating food contaminated by pathogens or chemical toxins**

2. CDC: **acronym for Centers for Disease Control & Prevention whose goal is improving public health**

3. pathogens: **a bacteria, virus, or other microorganism capable of causing disease**

4. inoculate: **introducing a toxic agent or a helpful vaccine into an organism**

5. stools: **human feces; poop**

6. culture: **growing of pathogens in lab to determine organism and sensitivity**

7. antitoxin: **an antibody capable of neutralizing a specific toxin**

8. salmonella: **gram-negative rod-shaped bacteria that causes food-borne illness by fecal contamination of food or water**

9. norovirus: **common foodborne pathogen causing 'stomach flu'; strikes quickly but typically resolves in 2-3 days**

10. toxoplasmosis: **parasitic infection transmitted through undercooked meat, or from soil or cat feces**

11. Department of Health: **the place where foodborne illness is reported by physicians**

12. food preparation guidelines: **safe steps for food preparation, handling, storage, and cooking**

Vocabulary 2: Matching

Directions: Match the definitions on the right to the terms on the left.

1. __D__ food-borne illness

2. __H__ CDC

3. __C__ pathogens

4. __I__ inoculate

5. __L__ stools

6. __B__ culture

7. __G__ antitoxin

8. __K__ salmonella

9. __A__ norovirus

10. __F__ toxoplasmosis

11. __J__ Department of Health

12. __E__ food preparation guidelines

a. common foodborne pathogen causing 'stomach flu'; strikes quickly but typically resolves in 2-3 days

b. growing of pathogens in lab to determine organism and sensitivity

c. a bacteria, virus, or other microorganism capable of causing disease

d. food poisoning; illness resulting from eating food contaminated by pathogens or chemical toxins

e. safe steps for food preparation, handling, storage, and cooking

f. parasitic infection transmitted through undercooked meat, or from soil or cat feces

g. an antibody capable of neutralizing a specific toxin

h. acronym for Centers for Disease Control & Prevention whose goal is improving public health

i. introducing a toxic agent or a helpful vaccine into an organism

j. the place where foodborne illness is reported by physicians

k. gram-negative rod-shaped bacteria that causes food-borne illness by fecal contamination of food or water

l. human feces; poop

Investigation 3.11A

Food-borne Illness

Vocabulary 3: Sentences

Dr. _____

P._____Date_____

Directions: Use each term in a sentence.

1. Food-borne illness: _____

_____

2. CDC:_____

_____

3. pathogens: _____

_____

4. inoculate: _____

_____

5. stools: _____

_____

6. culture: _____

_____

7. antitoxin: _____

_____

8. salmonella: _____

_____

9. norovirus: _____

_____

10. toxoplasmosis: _____

_____

11. Department of Health: _____

_____

12. food preparation guidelines: _____

_____

Foodborne Pathogens Worksheet

Directions: Refer to your reading in Foodborne Pathogens to answer the following questions.

1. Foodborne Illness is commonly called **food poisoning**.

2. To what U.S. government agency does the acronym "CDC" refer?

   Centers for Disease Control and Prevention

3. About how many foodborne diseases are recognized by the CDC? **> 250**

4. What are the three major categories of foodborne illness?

   a. **bacterial**

   b. **viral**

   c. **parasitic**

5. What fraction of the total U.S. population gets food poisoning each year?
   1 / 6

6. About how many people die from foodborne illnesses each year in the U.S.?
   3,000

7. Name five bacterial foodborne illnesses.

   a. **Staph Aureus**   (any five)

   b. **Campylobacter**

   c. **E. Coli**

   d. **Listeria**

   e. **Salmonella**   **(also Botulism)**

8. What virus causes the most foodborne illness in the U.S.?

   Norovirus

9. How can anyone insure they do not contract hepatitis A?

   vaccination is available to prevent hepatitis A and B

10. Why is it important for the physician to know which bacteria is causing the illness?

    The treatment for the infection depends on the organism causing the illness. Also, physicians must report cases of foodborne illness to the health department.

11. What is often the best test available to determine the pathogen causing the foodborne illness?

    stool sample microscopic exam and culture

12. What is the Mice Inoculation Test used for?

    testing for botulism

13. What are the four basic rules of safe food preparation?

    a. Clean: wash your hands and working surfaces often

    b. Separate: keep meat separate from fruits and vegetables in your prep area

    c. Cook: don't eat undercooked foods, especially meats

    d. Chill: refrigerate perishable foods immediately – don't let them sit out at room temperature

14. Name two ways that bacteria and parasites are similar.

    a. **one-celled organisms**   **microscopic**

    b. **living**   **can cause illness**   (any two)

15. Name three responsibilities physicians have in caring for their patients

    a. **ask questions & listen closely to the answers**

    b. **order appropriate tests**

    c. **educate patients about preventive measures in food preparation**

Food-borne Pathogen Case

Vocabulary 1: Definitions

Directions: Use the text, a dictionary, or the internet to write a definition for each term.

1. abdominal cramps: **stomach pain**

2. diarrhea: **condition where feces discharged in liquid form**

3. vomiting: **emesis, regurgitation, or throwing up; stomach contents ejected through mouth or nose**

4. fever: **an elevation of body temperature often signaling an infection; pyrexia**

5. joint pain: **pain limited to your shoulder, your knee, your elbow, and so on**

6. food-borne pathogen: **any bacteria, virus, fungi, or parasite capable of causing illness when ingested in food or water**

7. antibiotic: **medicine that inhibits the growth or kills bacteria**

8. pathogenic parasite: **any parasite with the potential to cause illness; examples are toxoplasma and trichinella**

9. pathogenic virus: **a virus having the capability of causing illness, such as norovirus & hepatitis A**

10. pathogenic bacteria: **any bacteria capable of causing illness, such as staph aureus or salmonella**

11. stool specimen: **a poop sample; a tool for determining the cause of foodborne illness**

12. dehydrated: **condition with loss of 5% or more of your body fluid**

Investigation 3.11B

Food-borne Pathogen Case

Vocabulary 2: Matching

Directions: Match the definitions on the right to the terms on the left.

1. __C__ abdominal cramps

2. __F__ diarrhea

3. __H__ vomiting

4. __B__ fever

5. __E__ joint pain

6. __J__ food-borne pathogen

7. __K__ antibiotic

8. __I__ pathogenic parasite

9. __A__ pathogenic virus

10. __L__ pathogenic bacteria

11. __D__ stool specimen

12. __G__ dehydrated

a. a virus having the capability of causing illness, such as norovirus & hepatitis A

b. an elevation of body temperature often signaling an infection; pyrexia

c. stomach pain

d. a poop sample; a tool for determining the cause of foodborne illness

e. pain limited to your shoulder, your knee, your elbow, and so on

f. condition where feces discharged in liquid form

g. condition with loss of 5% or more of your body fluid

h. emesis, regurgitation, or throwing up; stomach contents ejected through mouth or nose

i. any parasite with the potential to cause illness; examples are toxoplasma and trichinella

j. any bacteria, virus, fungi, or parasite capable of causing illness when ingested in food or water

k. medicine that inhibits the growth or kills bacteria

l. any bacteria capable of causing illness, such as staph aureus or salmonella

Investigation 3.11B

Food-borne Pathogen Case

Vocabulary 3: Sentences

Dr. _____

P._____Date_____

Directions: Write a sentence using each term.

1. abdominal cramps: _____

    _____

2. diarrhea:_____

    _____

3. vomiting: _____

    _____

4. fever: _____

    _____

5. joint pain: _____

    _____

6. food-borne pathogen: _____

    _____

7. antibiotic: _____

    _____

8. pathogenic parasite: _____

    _____

9. pathogenic virus: _____

    _____

10. pathogenic bacteria: _____

    _____

11. stool specimen: _____

    _____

12. dehydrated: _____

    _____

3.11B: Foodborne Pathogens

Foodborne Pathogen Case

1. What are Grace's symptoms of her illness?

    a. **abdominal cramps**

    b. **diarrhea**

    c. **vomiting**

    d. **fever**

    e. **joint pain**

2. Which clues helped direct you to consider foodborne illness as the origin of Grace's sickness? (any three)

    a. **boyfriend had same symptoms coming on at same time**

    b. **chicken left out at room temperature for hours**

    c. **patient reports chicken did not look completely cooked**

    d. **patient's symptoms consistent with those expected in foodborne illness**

3. What was unusual about the timing of Grace's and her boyfriend's becoming sick?

    both came down with same symptoms at exactly the same time

4. Which two bacteria are candidates as the most likely pathogen in Grace's illness?

    a. **Salmonella**

    b. **Campylobacter**

5. How are the two most likely bacterial pathogens treated differently?

    Salmonella is NOT treated with antibiotics

    Campylobacter IS treated with antibiotics

6. Which test can you perform to identify the actual pathogen in this case?

    stool sample microscopic exam + send to lab for culture & sensitivity test

7. The results of the stool sample test identify the pathogen as Salmonella. What should you do now?

> **Recommend rest and drink fluids. Do NOT prescribe antibiotics**
>
> **Patient should call you back if not better in 5 – 7 days**

8. Should you contact any public agency to report this food poisoning event?

   Circle your answer: **YES**   NO

9. If yes, which agency should be contacted and why? If no, why not?

> **Local Health Department or CDC should be contacted so they can investigate**
>
> **the source of the infection to perhaps prevent others from illness**

This case represents a dangerous habit many people display: leaving perishable foods without refrigeration for extended periods of time. Two good habits pertaining to pre-cooked chickens are:

1. **Make sure the chicken is fully cooked; don't pick the lightest chicken in the batch. Also, look at the time stamp on the chicken; select one that has not been sitting out more than one hour.**
2. **When you get the chicken home, place it in the refrigerator immediately if you are not able to eat it right away.**

Follow-up: As Grace's physician, you would call Grace to give her the results of the laboratory test. In this case you would also advise her that antibiotics are not recommended for this particular bacteria. You would then advise her that Salmonella illness usually lasts 5 to 7 days, and ask her to contact you if she does not feel better in a few more days because Salmonella in some people can revolve into a more serious condition.

Crossword   **Foodborne Illness**

Directions: Use the highlighted terms in the chapter to solve the puzzle. Most clues come from the chapter text, some require outside investigation. Omit spaces or dashes between words.

Solution:

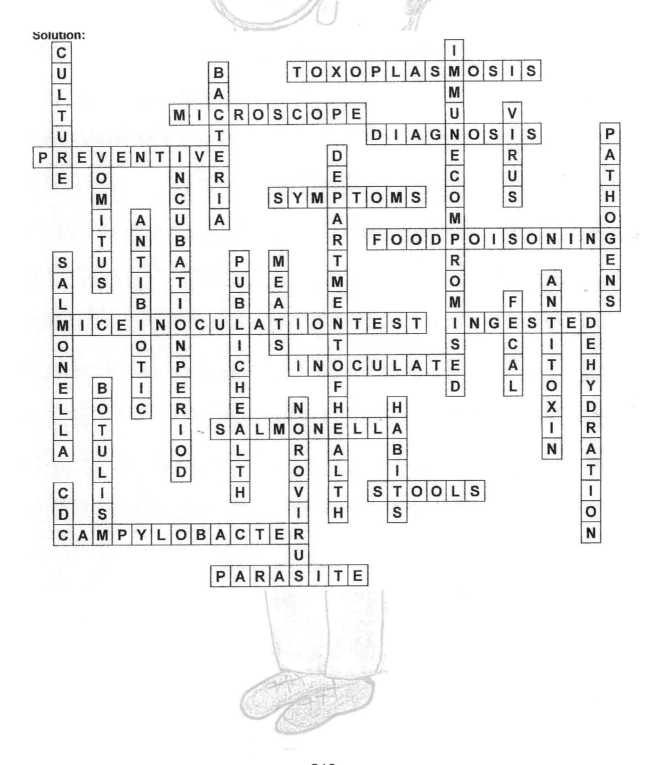

Head Injury

Vocabulary 1: Definitions

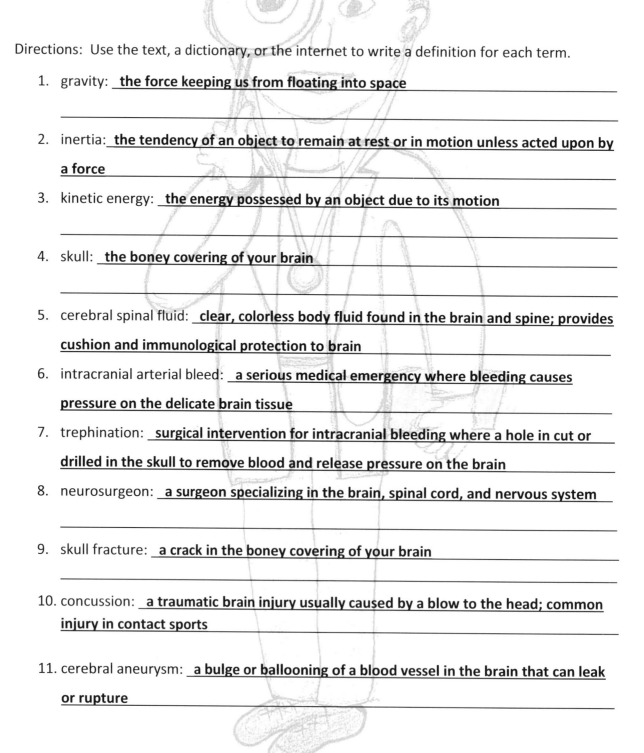

Directions: Use the text, a dictionary, or the internet to write a definition for each term.

1. gravity: __the force keeping us from floating into space__

2. inertia: __the tendency of an object to remain at rest or in motion unless acted upon by a force__

3. kinetic energy: __the energy possessed by an object due to its motion__

4. skull: __the boney covering of your brain__

5. cerebral spinal fluid: __clear, colorless body fluid found in the brain and spine; provides cushion and immunological protection to brain__

6. intracranial arterial bleed: __a serious medical emergency where bleeding causes pressure on the delicate brain tissue__

7. trephination: __surgical intervention for intracranial bleeding where a hole in cut or drilled in the skull to remove blood and release pressure on the brain__

8. neurosurgeon: __a surgeon specializing in the brain, spinal cord, and nervous system__

9. skull fracture: __a crack in the boney covering of your brain__

10. concussion: __a traumatic brain injury usually caused by a blow to the head; common injury in contact sports__

11. cerebral aneurysm: __a bulge or ballooning of a blood vessel in the brain that can leak or rupture__

Head Injury

Vocabulary 2: Matching

Directions: Match the definitions on the right to the medical terms on the left.

1. __B__ gravity

2. __J__ inertia

3. __H__ kinetic energy

4. __C__ skull

5. __K__ cerebral spinal fluid

6. __E__ intracranial arterial bleed

7. __I__ trephination

8. __A__ neurosurgeon

9. __D__ skull fracture

10. __G__ concussion

11. __F__ cerebral aneurysm

a. a surgeon specializing in the brain, spinal cord, and nervous system

b. the force keeping us from floating into space

c. the boney covering of your brain

d. a crack in the boney covering of your brain

e. a serious medical emergency where bleeding causes pressure on the delicate brain tissue

f. a bulge or ballooning of a blood vessel in the brain that can leak or rupture

g. a traumatic brain injury usually caused by a blow to the head; common injury in contact sports

h. the energy possessed by an object due to its motion

i. surgical intervention for intracranial bleeding where a hole in cut or drilled in the skull to remove blood and release pressure on the brain

j. the tendency of an object to remain at rest or in motion unless acted upon by a force

k. clear, colorless body fluid found in the brain and spine; provides cushion and immunological protection to brain

Investigation 3.12A

Head Injury

Vocabulary 3: Sentences

Dr. _____

P._____Date_____

Directions: Use each term in a sentence.

1. gravity: _____

    _____

2. inertia:_____

    _____

3. kinetic energy: _____

    _____

4. skull: _____

    _____

5. cerebral spinal fluid: _____

    _____

6. intracranial arterial bleed: _____

    _____

7. trephination: _____

    _____

8. neurosurgeon: _____

    _____

9. skull fracture: _____

    _____

10. concussion: _____

    _____

11. cerebral aneurysm: _____

    _____

Head Injury

1. As you approached Alice and the other players untangled themselves and moved away, what three positive signs did you observe in Alice's condition?

   a. **No blood is visible**

   b. **Signs of breathing are visible**

   c. **No one is crying out in pain**

2. As you quickly visually examined Alice as she lay on the floor, what things did you observe that concerned you?

   a. **Alice is not moving or speaking**

   b. **She appears to have a broken leg**

   c. **Her pupils are dilated and not reacting to light**

3. Why didn't you take a complete history on this patient?

   She was not conscious

4. What were Alice's vital signs when taken by Liz and Graham?

   BP = **190/88** mmHg   Pulse = **140** beats/min   Respirations = **24** breaths/min

5. What is the normal range for resting blood pressure? **90-120 /60-80** mmHg

6. What is the normal pulse range for an athlete like Alice?   **40 to 80** beats/min

7. What might explain Alice's blood pressure at the time it was taken following her injury?

   Alice was playing an intense game of basketball.

8. **Do you think** the change in Alice's blood pressure could have triggered the bleeding in her brain? Why or Why Not?

YES   NO   Why: **Strenuous activities such as competitive basketball require more blood be pumped throughout the body. This requires the heart to beat faster. A faster beating heart sends more blood through the arteries, which raises the pressure. The increased blood pressure placed extra stress on the aneurysm in her brain, which ruptured from the excess pressure.**

9. What is an aneurysm?

   An aneurysm is a localized enlargement of an artery caused by weakening of the arterial wall.

10. What is a cerebral aneurysm?

    A weak or thin area in a blood vessel within the brain that bulges out and places increased pressure on the brain. It can rupture, causing a brain bleed, which requires emergency treatment.

11. Do you think there could be any significance to the shaking of Alice's body that was observed while the bodies were still entangled on the floor? If so, what?

    Yes. The shaking of Alice's body could well have been the result of her suffering a seizure related to the sudden bleeding and change of pressure inside her skull.

12. Why did you think it was necessary to quickly transport Alice to the hospital and have a neurosurgeon ready to examine her on arrival?

    a. **Alice was not conscious**

    b. **Alice's eyes were dilated and not responsive to light**

13. What simple test can be performed to indicate whether or not a patient has probably sustained a bleeding event inside their skull that is putting pressure on the brain? How is the test performed?

    Check their eyes to see if the pupils are excessively dilated. If you have a flashlight you can alternately focus the light beam on the eye and then away; the pupil size should get smaller with light shined and larger when the light is directed away from the eye.

14. If the Pupil Reaction Test is positive in both eyes, meaning both pupils are fixed in dilation and not reactive to light, what does that most likely indicate in this patient? **It indicates the brain injury is to the area of the brain affecting sight to both eyes**

15. What is the name of the area, or lobe, of the brain that controls vision?

    Occipital Lobe

16. Does it always mean there is potential brain damage if both eyes are fixed in a dilated state? Think about the last time you had a complete eye examination; did they do anything to your eyes?

    No. Eyes can be dilated temporarily by drugs or medicines. Police look in the eyes of suspected drug users to help screen them for being under the influence. Eye doctors dilate the eyes using medicines that allow them to thoroughly examine your eyes.

17. Which two physician specialists from the list probably encounter the stress of treating emergencies most often?

    1. **Emergency Room Physician**   2. **Trauma Surgeon**

18. You have had time to think about the level of stress you would enjoy dealing with in your medical career. Which specialty or specialties appeal most at this time to your sense of your desire and ability to deal with stress? (**any student response**)

    1. _____   2. _____

19. Looking back at your previous thoughts about how often various doctors encounter emergency situations, circle the frequency you think each of the following medical specialists encounter emergencies, where clear thinking and swift action is required.

Rare	**Occasional**	Common	CARDIOLOGIST
Rare	Occasional	Common	DERMATOLOGIST
Rare	Occasional	**Common**	EMERGENCY ROOM PHYSICIAN
Rare	**Occasional**	Common	OBSTETRICIAN
Rare	Occasional	Common	PATHOLOGIST
Rare	Occasional	Common	PODIATRIST
Rare	**Occasional**	Common	ANESTHESIOLOGIST
Rare	Occasional	**Common**	ORTHOPEDIST
Rare	**Occasional**	Common	OPTHAMOLOGIST
Rare	Occasional	**Common**	TRAUMA SURGEON

3.12 - Activity 1: Checking Pupil Reactivity

Required Supplies: Penlight or Flashlight (not a laser)

Directions: Follow the steps in order:

1. Lower the light level in the room if possible
2. Get a partner to test
3. Observe the pupil size of your test subject; both pupils should be approximately equal in size
4. Quickly shine the penlight or flashlight briefly (1 or 2 seconds) into their eye and observe the pupil constrict (get smaller)
5. Then shine the light away from the eye and watch the pupil get larger.
6. Repeat steps four (4) and five (5) on the other eye
7. What happened when you shined the light in your partner's eye?
   both pupils constrict (get smaller) when light shone in either eye and get larger when light turned off

Investigation 3.12A Head Injury

Post-Script

Alice made it to the hospital emergency room and the neurosurgeon was waiting and ready to take over. He performed neurological tests and determined that Alice was, indeed, in danger of permanent brain damage if he did not relieve the pressure on her brain. He ordered that she be delivered immediately to the special procedures room so that he can perform emergency brain surgery.

Thanks to your medical curiosity about Alice's condition and your medical knowledge to know first, to look at her eyes, and second, to know the significance of her eyes appearing fixed and dilated, Alice came through her surgery well and suffered no permanent disabilities.

Do you think you might want to be a brain surgeon? Later in this chapter you will come across some activities you can use to find out.

Crossword 3.12A   **Head Injury**

Directions: Use the highlighted terms in the chapter to solve the puzzle. Most clues come from the chapter text, some require outside investigation. Omit spaces or dashes between words.

Solution:

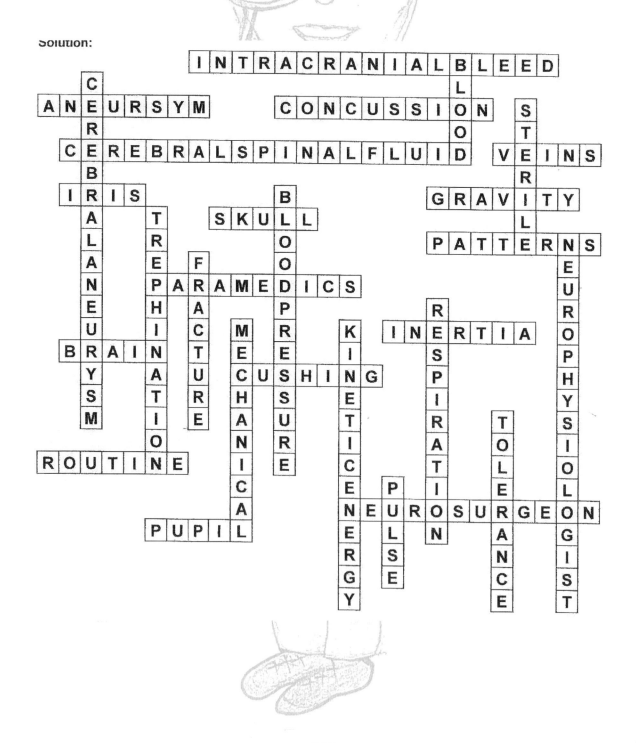

The Eye

Vocabulary 1A: Definitions

Directions: Use the text, a dictionary, or the internet to write a definition for each term.

1. cornea: __the transparent layer forming the front of the eye__

2. transparent: __allowing light to pass through such that objects behind can be seen__

3. astigmatism: __a misshaped eyeball that isn't round enough, but instead too egg-shaped to properly focus light evenly__

4. Lasik: __laser vision correction for myopia, hyperopia, and astigmatism__

5. myopia: __visual defect where light is focused in front of the retina; nearsightedness__

6. hyperopia: __an eye defect where light focuses behind the retina; farsightedness__

7. corneal abrasion: __a scratch on the cornea of the eye__

8. iris: __the round area behind the cornea that adjusts the opening of the pupil and gives eyes their color__

9. pupil: __the black area inside the iris that regulates the amount of light entering the eye__

10. lens: __it focuses the light rays passing through it onto the retina and changes the focal distance by changing shape__

11. cataract: __a condition where the eye's lens becomes progressively opaque, resulting in blurred vision__

12. bifocals: __eyeglasses or contact lens having two areas, one for near and one for far vision__

Investigation 3.12B

The Eye

Vocabulary 2A: Matching

Directions: Match the definitions on the right to the medical terms on the left.

1. __I__ cornea

2. __E__ transparent

3. __L__ astigmatism

4. __A__ Lasik

5. __K__ myopia

6. __D__ hyperopia

7. __J__ corneal abrasion

8. __G__ iris

9. __C__ pupil

10. __F__ lens

11. __H__ cataract

12. __B__ bifocals

a. laser vision correction for myopia, hyperopia, and astigmatism

b. eyeglasses or contact lens having two areas, one for near and one for far vision

c. the black area inside the iris that regulates the amount of light entering the eye

d. an eye defect where light focuses behind the retina; farsightedness

e. allowing light to pass through such that objects behind can be seen

f. it focuses the light rays passing through it onto the retina and changes the focal distance by changing shape

g. the round area behind the cornea that adjusts the opening of the pupil and gives eyes their color

h. a condition where the eye's lens becomes progressively opaque, resulting in blurred vision

i. the transparent layer forming the front of the eye

j. a scratch on the cornea of the eye

k. visual defect where light is focused in front of the retina; nearsightedness

l. a misshaped eyeball that isn't round enough, but instead too egg-shaped to properly focus light evenly

Investigation 3.12B

Dr. _____

The Eye

P._____Date_____

Vocabulary 3A: Sentences

Directions: Use each term in a sentence.

1. cornea: _____

    _____

2. transparent:_____

    _____

3. astigmatism: _____

    _____

4. Lasik: _____

    _____

5. myopia:__ _____

    _____

6. hyperopia: _____

    _____

7. corneal abrasion: _____

    _____

8. iris:_____ _____

    _____

9. pupil:_____

    _____

10. lens: _____

    _____

11. cataract: _____

    _____

12. bifocals: _____

    _____

The Eye

Vocabulary 1B: Definitions

Directions: Use the text, a dictionary, or the internet to write a definition for each term.

1. progressive: **happening or developing gradually, or proceeding step by step**

2. retina: **the layer at the back of the eye where the visual image forms**

3. rods: **the photoreceptors in the retina responsible for vision at low light levels in only black and white**

4. cones: **photoreceptors in the retina responsible for color vision**

5. detached retina: **condition where retina becomes separated from underlying tissue, causing loss of vision in affected area**

6. ophthalmoscope: **an instrument for examining the retina and other parts of the eye**

7. macula: **the area of the retina most packed with cones and having the keenest vision**

8. macular degeneration: **an age-related degenerative eye condition affecting the central part of the retina resulting in distortion or loss of vision**

9. optic nerve : **second pair of cranial nerves, transmits impulses from retina to brain**

10. glaucoma: **a condition of increased pressure within the eyeball that causes gradual loss of vision**

11. thalamus: **brain matter that acts as relay of left and right eye visual input**

12. occipital lobe: **the brain lobe responsible for processing visual input**

Investigation 3.12B

The Eye

Vocabulary 2B: Matching

Directions: Match the definitions on the right to the medical terms on the left.

1. __I__ progressive

2. __A__ retina

3. __K__ rods

4. __G__ cones

5. __C__ detached retina

6. __B__ ophthalmoscope

7. __J__ macula

8. __L__ macular degeneration

9. __E__ optic nerve

10. __H__ glaucoma

11. __D__ thalamus

12. __F__ occipital lobe

a. the layer at the back of the eye where the visual image forms

b. an instrument for examining the retina and other parts of the eye

c. condition where retina becomes separated from underlying tissue, causing loss of vision in affected area

d. brain matter that acts as relay of left and right eye visual input

e. second pair of cranial nerves, transmits impulses from retina to brain

f. the brain lobe responsible for processing visual input

g. photoreceptors in the retina responsible for color vision

h. a condition of increased pressure within the eyeball that causes gradual loss of vision

i. happening or developing gradually, or proceeding step by step

j. the area of the retina most packed with cones and having the keenest vision

k. the photoreceptors in the retina responsible for vision at low light levels in only black and white

l. an age-related degenerative eye condition affecting the central part of the retina resulting in distortion or loss of vision

Investigation 3.12B

The Eye

Dr. _____

P_____Date_____

Vocabulary 3B: Sentences

Directions: Use each term in a sentence.

1. progressive: _____
   _____

2. retina:_____
   _____

3. rods: _____
   _____

4. cones: _____
   _____

5. detached retina: _____
   _____

6. ophthalmoscope: _____
   _____

7. macula: _____
   _____

8. macular degeneration: _____
   _____

9. optic nerve : _____
   _____

10. glaucoma:_____
    _____

11. thalamus: _____
    _____

12. occipital lobe: _____
    _____

The Eye

Directions: Answer the following questions about the eye.

1. What is the pupil? **The pupil is the hole in the center of the eye through which light passes.**

2. What is the iris? **The iris is the pigmented part of the eye that dilates and contracts with changes in light.**

3. What is the function of the iris? **The function of the iris is to constrict in bright light, allowing less light into the pupil, and dilate in dim light, allowing more of the light into the iris.**

4. What is the eye lens? **The lens is the clear structure behind the iris.**

5. What is the function of your lens **The function of the lens is to focus the image onto the retina.**

6. How does the lens focus both close and far away objects? **? The lens changes shape to bring objects into focus depending on their distance from the eye.**

7. Why do people over age 40 often wear reading glasses or bifocal glasses for near and far sight? **After around age 40 the lens becomes brittle and loses its ability to change shape. Visual clarity is lost to either near or far vision, or both.**

8. What eye structure protects the lens from being easily scratched when we rub our eyes? What else does it do? **The cornea protects the eye. It is also responsible to help bend light into the lens.**

9. What is the cornea? **The cornea is the thin, clear outer covering of the eye.**

10. What common injury occurs to the cornea? **a scratched cornea**

11. What is the retina? **The retina is the thin, light-sensitive membrane lining the inner eyeball. It is like the movie screen of the eye. Light travels through the cornea, pupil, and lens, and is then focused into an image on the retina.**

12. Name two types of specialized cells located on the retina? Describe their functions.

    Rods: photoreceptor cells used for peripheral vision in less intense light

    Cones: photoreceptor cells responsible for our color vision; work best in brighter light

13. In what orientation do images appear on our retinas?

    Images are oriented upside down on the retina.

14. Where do the upside-down images seem to get turned right side up?

    Images are inverted to their proper orientation in the brain.

15. Name two common injuries that occur to the retina, mostly in people past age 50?

    a. **detached retina**

    b. **macular degeneration**

16. How does an image move from the retina to your brain?

    It travels via the optic nerves to the occipital lobe of the brain.

17. How might an injury to the back of the head cause impaired vision or a ruptured aneurysm result in fixed and dilated pupils? **An injury to the back of the head or ruptured aneurysm in the occipital lobe would cause vision problems or dilated pupils because of swelling of or pressure on the brain in that area which might interrupt the transmission of signals along the optic nerves.**

Crossword 3.12B   **The Eye**

Directions: Use the highlighted terms in the chapter to solve the puzzle. Most clues come from the chapter text, some require outside investigation. Omit spaces or dashes between words.

Solution:

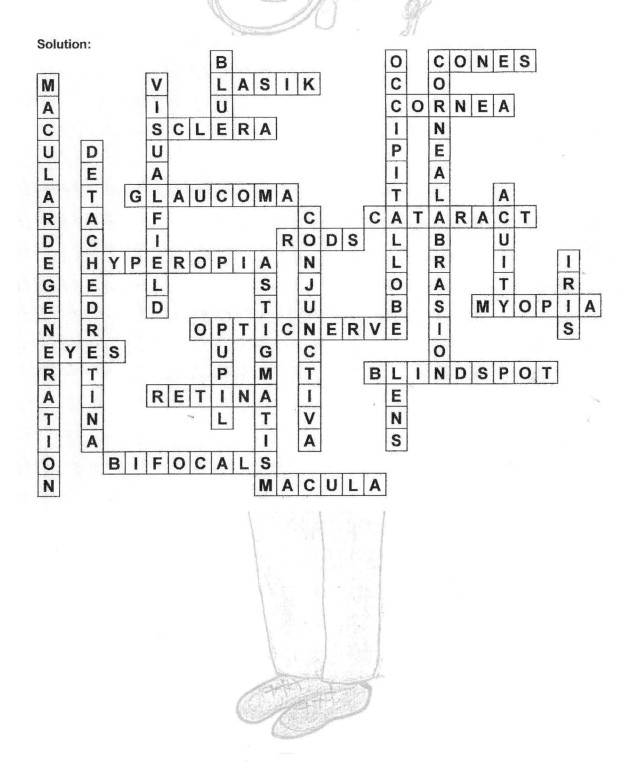

The Brain

Vocabulary 1A: Definitions

Directions: Use the text, a dictionary, or the internet to write a definition for each term.

1. neuroanatomist: __the scientist who studies the anatomy and organization of the__
__nervous system__

2. gross:__ large enough to be visualized with only the naked eye__

3. hemisphere: __the left or right half of the brain, connected by the corpus callosum__

4. lobes: __the divisions of the cerebrum of our brain in four distinct functional areas__

5. neural plasticity: __the brain's neurons ability to learn and adapt to an individual's__
__needs regardless of their place within the brain__

6. neurons: __specialized cells that transmit nerve impulses in the brain and throughout__
__the body__

7. neurologist: __a physician who specializes in treating diseases of the nervous system__

8. stroke: __the sudden death of brain cells caused by blockage of blood flow or rupture of__
__an artery in the brain__

9. frontal lobe: __the area of the brain lying directly behind the forehead__

10. parietal lobes: __lobes positioned above the occipital lobes serving as the highest level__
__of sensory and motor awareness__

11. cortical homunculus: __the sensory and motor neurological maps of the anatomical__
__divisions of the body located in the brain__

12. sensation: __a feeling or perception of motion or sensation of contact with the body__

The Brain

Vocabulary 2A: Matching

Directions: Match the definitions on the right to the terms on the left.

1. __E__ neuroanatomist

2. __L__ gross

3. __C__ hemisphere

4. __H__ lobes

5. __J__ neural plasticity

6. __F__ neurons

7. __B__ neurologist

8. __K__ stroke

9. __D__ frontal lobe

10. __G__ parietal lobes

11. __A__ cortical homunculus

12. __I__ sensation

a. the sensory and motor neurological maps of the anatomical divisions of the body located in the brain

b. a physician who specializes in treating diseases of the nervous system

c. the left or right half of the brain, connected by the corpus callosum

d. the area of the brain lying directly behind the forehead

e. the scientist who studies the anatomy and organization of the nervous system

f. specialized cells that transmit nerve impulses in the brain and throughout the body

g. lobes positioned above the occipital lobes serving as the highest level of sensory and motor awareness

h. the divisions of the cerebrum of our brain in four distinct functional areas

i. a feeling or perception of motion or sensation of contact with the body

j. the brain's neurons ability to learn and adapt to an individual's needs regardless of their place within the brain

k. the sudden death of brain cells caused by blockage of blood flow or rupture of an artery in the brain

l. large enough to be visualized with only the naked eye

Investigation 3.13A

The Brain

Vocabulary 3A: Sentences

Dr. _____

P._____Date_____

Directions: Use each term in a sentence.

1. neuroanatomist: _____

_____

2. gross:_____

_____

3. hemisphere: _____

_____

4. lobes: _____

_____

5. neural plasticity: _____

_____

6. neurons: _____

_____

7. neurologist: _____

_____

8. stroke: _____

_____

9. frontal lobe: _____

_____

10. parietal lobes: _____

_____

11. cortical homunculus: _____

_____

12. sensation: _____

_____

The Brain

Vocabulary 1B: Definitions

Directions: Use the text, a dictionary, or the internet to write a definition for each term.

1. motor: __having to do with motion or action; example: stimulating a muscle to contract__

2. temporal lobe: __the area of the brain located above your ears receiving sensory information about sounds and understanding speech__

3. occipital lobe: __the visual processing center of our brain__

4. cerebellum: __the area of the brain responsible for coordination of muscular activity__

5. coordination: __the ability to use various parts of the body together smoothly and efficiently__

6. brain stem: __the part of the brain controlling and regulating vital body functions including respiration, heart rate, and blood pressure__

7. action potential: __nerve impulses that stimulate a change in another neuron or cause a muscle cell to contract__

8. axons: __the long threadlike portion of a neuron that conducts impulses from the cell body to other neurons__

9. dendrites: __short neuron extensions that receive impulses from axons at synapses and transmit to the cell body__

10. inhibition: __a feeling of restraint or blockage; blocking an impulse or limiting an action__

11. backpropogation: __adjusting a system by comparing to desired output and adjusting until difference is minimized__

12. artificial intelligence: __the use of computer systems to perform tasks normally requiring human intelligence__

Investigation 3.13A

The Brain

Vocabulary 2B: Matching

Directions: Match the definitions on the right to the terms on the left.

1. __D__   motor

2. __B__   temporal lobe

3. __I__   occipital lobe

4. __G__   cerebellum

5. __E__   coordination

6. __K__   brain stem

7. __A__   action potential

8. __H__   axon

9. __L__   dendrites

10. __C__   inhibition

11. __J__   backpropagation

12. __F__   artificial intelligence

a. nerve impulses that stimulate a change in another neuron or cause a muscle cell to contract

b. the area of the brain located above your ears receiving sensory information about sounds and understanding speech

c. a feeling of restraint or blockage; blocking an impulse or limiting an action

d. having to do with motion or action; example: stimulating a muscle to contract

e. the ability to use various parts of the body together smoothly and efficiently

f. the use of computer systems to perform tasks normally requiring human intelligence

g. the area of the brain responsible for coordination of muscular activity

h. the long threadlike portion of a neuron that conducts impulses from the cell body to other neurons

i. the visual processing center of our brain

j. adjusting a system by comparing to desired output and adjusting until difference is minimized

k. the part of the brain controlling and regulating vital body functions including respiration, heart rate, and blood pressure

l. short neuron extensions that receive impulses from axons at synapses and transmit to the cell body

Investigation 3.13A

Dr. _____

The Brain

P. _____ Date _____

Vocabulary 3B: Sentences

Directions: Use each term in a sentence.

1. motor: _____
_____

2. temporal lobe: _____
_____

3. occipital lobe: _____
_____

4. cerebellum: _____
_____

5. coordination: _____
_____

6. brain stem: _____
_____

7. action potential: _____
_____

8. axons: _____
_____

9. dendrites: _____
_____

10. inhibition: _____
_____

11. backpropogation: _____
_____

12. artificial intelligence: _____
_____

The Brain

Directions: Answer the following questions based on your reading of chapter 3.13A.

1. What does an 'anatomist' study?

   Scientists who study all aspects of the human structure

2. What does a 'neuroanatomist' study?

   Scientists who specialize in the study of the brain

3. What name describes the two sides of your brain?

   hemispheres

4. Each brain hemisphere contains how many lobes?

   four

5. Name the lobes of your cerebral cortex:

   a. **frontal**

   b. **temporal**

   c. **parietal**

   d. **occipital**

6. What name do we give the ability of the brain regain normal function following major brain injury? **neural plasticity**

7. What signs should your recognize and attribute to a possible stroke?

   a. **rapid loss of speech**

   b. **loss of sensation or movement on one side of the body**

8. Which lobe of the brain controls your emotions, passions, and hopes?

   frontal lobe

9. What is the primary function of the Occipital Lobe?

   visual processing

10. Why does each parietal lobe contain <u>two</u> invisible diagrams of your entire body?

    one homunculus for sensation, the other for motor

Investigation 3.13A The Brain   Teacher

Worksheet 3.13A1, page 2

11. About what percent of the information collected by the retina is forwarded by optic

    nerve to the brain? **10 %**

12. Which brain area, not a lobe, bears responsibility for coordination of all muscle

    movement in your body? **cerebellum**

13. List at least three functions of the brain stem.

    a. **regulate heart rate**

    b. **regulate breathing**

    c. **regulate sleep patterns**

    d. **appetite and eating**

14. How many cells does your brain contain? **many billions** of cells in our brain

15. What is an "action potential"?

       a pulse of electrical current generated by a cell

16. Groups of neurons, along with their axons and dendrites, make up nerve systems

    known as **neural networks**

17. Briefly describe the concept of "backpropogation".

       the manner in which neurons decide how to adjust their sensitivity to a

       stimulus

18. Describe "artificial intelligence" (you can look it up on the internet)

       the ability of machines and robots to react to stimuli in such a way that they

       learn how best to respond to that same stimuli the next time

19. The symptoms of a stroke depend upon what area of the brain stops receiving blood

    flow and oxygen. Where would you look for a stroke that paralyzes the left arm?

    on the right side of the brain

20. Can you think of an evolutionary advantage for the cross wiring of the brain so the right

    hemisphere has primary control of the left side of the body?

    Provide protection to the organism from an injury sustained to one side. Cross-wiring

    would continue some control in spite of the injury to that side of the brain.

Worksheet 3.13A2

  Basic Brain Anatomy

Directions: Label the parts of the brain. Try to do it without looking at the previous diagram.

Compare your answers with the diagram and make any necessary corrections.

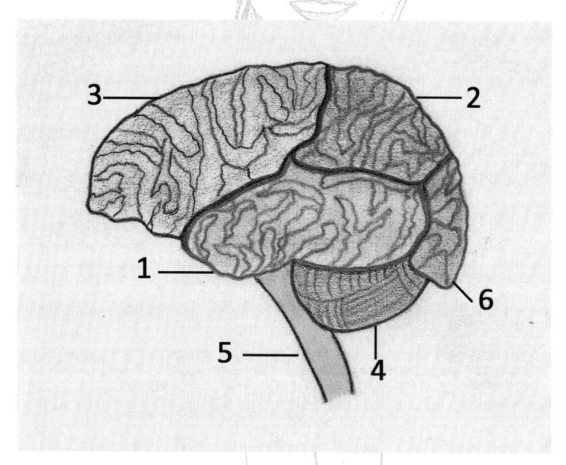

Directions: Write the name of the brain part corresponding to each number.

1. _____ TEMPORAL LOBE _____

2. _____ PARIETAL LOBE _____

3. _____ FRONTAL LOBE _____

4. _____ CEREBELLUM _____

5. _____ BRAIN STEM _____

6. _____ OCCIPITAL LOBE _____

Brain Worksheet 2

Right vs Left Brain Activity

Directions: Place an R in the space to identify Right Brain Activity. Place an L in the space to indicate a Left Brain Activity. Refer back to the diagram if needed.

L	Science & Math	**R**	Intuition
R	Music Awareness	**L**	Language
L	Numbers Skills	**L**	Logic
R	Imagination	**L**	Analytic thought
R	3-D Forms Visualization	**R**	Holistic thought
L	Right-hand control	**L**	Reasoning
R	Left-hand control	**R**	Art Awareness

The Brain

Directions: Use the highlighted terms in the chapter to solve the puzzle. Most clues come from the chapter text, some require outside investigation. Omit spaces or dashes between words.

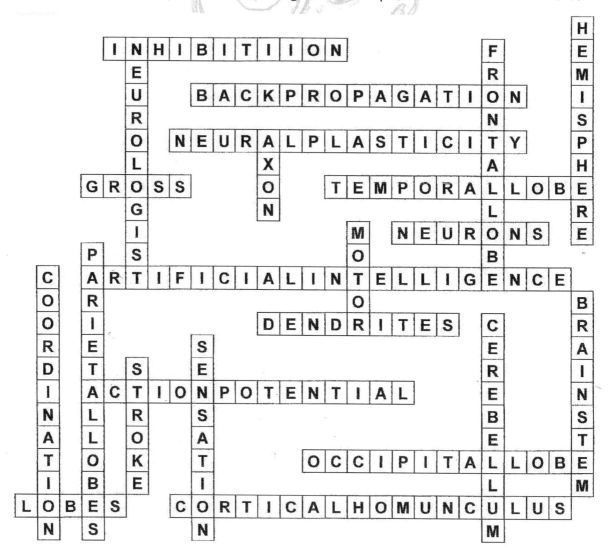

242

Crossword 3.13A2   The Brain

Directions: Use the highlighted terms in the chapter to solve the puzzle. Most clues come from the chapter text, some require outside investigation. Omit spaces or dashes between words.

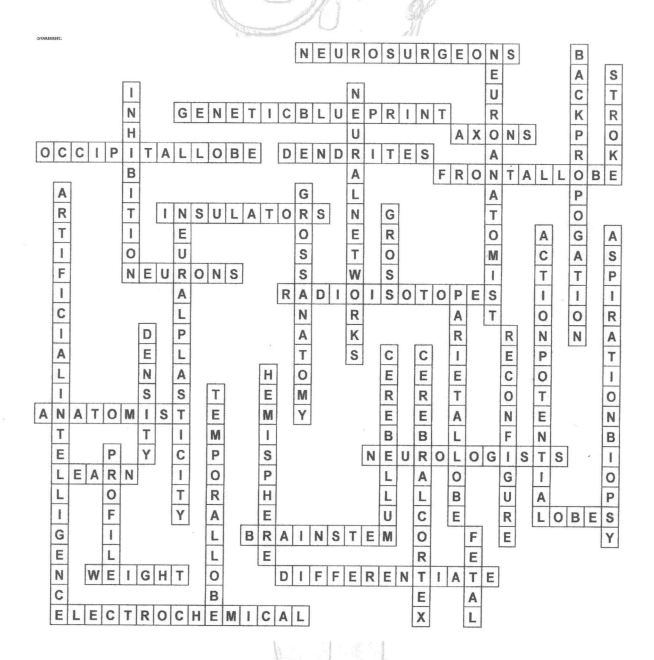

Normal or Abnormal?

Vocabulary 1: Definitions

Directions: Use the text, a dictionary, or the internet to write a definition for each term.

1. thermostat: __a control system having set inputs but no measure of the output__

2. **closed loop system:** __a control system that measures output, compares that measurement to the desired output, and uses the difference to dictate what happens next__

3. open loop system: __a controller that regulates or activates a device when temperature reaches a certain point__

4. extract: __to remove or utilize__

5. calories: __a unit of heat used to indicate the amount of energy foods will produce in the human body__

6. adaptive controllers: __advanced controllers capable of complex decision-making and capable of learning__

7. pacemaker: __electronic device implanted inside the body to control the heart rate__

8. conferences: __meetings attended by physicians to update their knowledge as part of their commitment to lifelong learning__

9. REM sleep: __rapid eye movement sleep that occurs at intervals where dreaming occurs and pulse, breathing, and movement increase__

10. Non-REM sleep: __the dreamless phase of sleep where breathing and heart rate are slow and regular__

11. Biological clock: __our innate mechanism that controls our individual timing and behaviors, and physiological states and processes__

12. metformin: __an oral medicine used to improve blood sugar control in type II diabetics by helping the body utilize insulin more efficiently__

Normal or Abnormal?

Vocabulary 2: Matching

Directions: Match the descriptions on the right to the terms on the left.

1. __B__ thermostat

2. __D__ closed loop system

3. __J__ open loop system

4. __I__ extract

5. __F__ calorie

6. __L__ adaptive controllers

7. __H__ pacemaker

8. __A__ conferences

9. __K__ REM sleep

10. __G__ non-REM sleep

11. __C__ biological clock

12. __E__ metformin

b. a control system having set inputs but no measure of the output

c. our innate mechanism that controls our individual timing and behaviors, and physiological states and processes

d. a control system that measures output, compares that measurement to the desired output, and uses the difference to dictate what happens next

e. an oral medicine used to improve blood sugar control in type II diabetics by helping the body utilize insulin more efficiently

f. a unit of heat used to indicate the amount of energy foods will produce in the human body

g. the dreamless phase of sleep where breathing and heart rate are slow and regular

h. electronic device implanted inside the body to control the heart rate

i. to remove or utilize

j. a controller that regulates or activates a device when temperature reaches a certain point

k. rapid eye movement sleep that occurs at intervals where dreaming occurs and pulse, breathing, and movement increase

l. advanced controllers capable of complex decision-making and capable of learning

a. meetings attended by physicians to update their knowledge as part of their commitment to lifelong learning

Normal or Abnormal?

Vocabulary 3: Sentences

Dr. _____

P. _____ Date _____

Directions: Use each term in a complete sentence.

1. thermostat: _____

_____

2. closed loop system: _____

_____

3. open loop system: _____

_____

4. extract: _____

_____

5. calories: _____

_____

6. adaptive controllers: _____

_____

7. pacemaker: _____

_____

8. conferences: _____

_____

9. REM sleep: _____

_____

10. Non-REM sleep: _____

_____

11. Biological clock: _____

_____

12. metformin: _____

_____

Reflections: Normal or Abnormal

Directions: Reflect on your reading of investigation 3.14A to answer the following questions.

1. Which area of the brain controls and regulates body temperature?

   hypothalamus

2. Which body system acts as our body's furnace?

   muscles

3. When our body extracts calories from food, into what is that energy converted?

   heat

4. Which specialty of medicine focuses on the ways the human body regulates itself and on diseases that affect that control?

   endocrinology

5. What electronic device is utilized to control the electrical impulses of the heart?

   pacemaker

6. What does any 'normal value' in the human body require?

   adaptive controllers

7. What are two purposes of sleep?

   a. **rest**

   b. **learning & long-term memory**

8. What are the two main categories of sleep?

   a. **REM sleep**

   b. **non-REM sleep**

9. During which phase of sleep do we dream?

   REM sleep

10. What special sleep-related skill do dolphins, porpoises, and penguins have?

They have the ability to sleep half their brain at a time, so they are always at least half awake.

11. Why do reptiles probably NOT dream about humans?

Reptiles do not appear to display REM sleep, which is required for dreaming.

12. The fact that we get tired and awake at pretty much the same time each day is related to the functioning of our **biological clock**.

13. Name four types of life events that can cause disruption of our sleep cycle.

a. **change in work schedule**

b. **medications**

c. **dietary change**

d. **travel across time zones**

14. What two conditions are necessary in order to maintain a healthy sleep schedule?

a. **a stable sleep schedule**

b. **a quiet, dark, comfortable bedroom**

15. Do you sleep well and feel rested most mornings? If yes, why do you think that happens? If no, which of the necessary conditions would you like to improve?

(student response)

_____

_____

_____

16. About how many years longer is the life expectancy for women longer than for men in the United States? **five** (5) years

17. Name two methods that may prove useful in extending lifespan.

a. **gene modification**

b. **preventing diseases**

18. Which country currently has the longest average lifespan? **Japan**

Crossword 3.13B   **Normal or Abnormal**

Directions: Use the highlighted terms in the chapter to solve the puzzle. Most clues come from the chapter text, some require outside investigation. Omit spaces or dashes between words.

Solution:

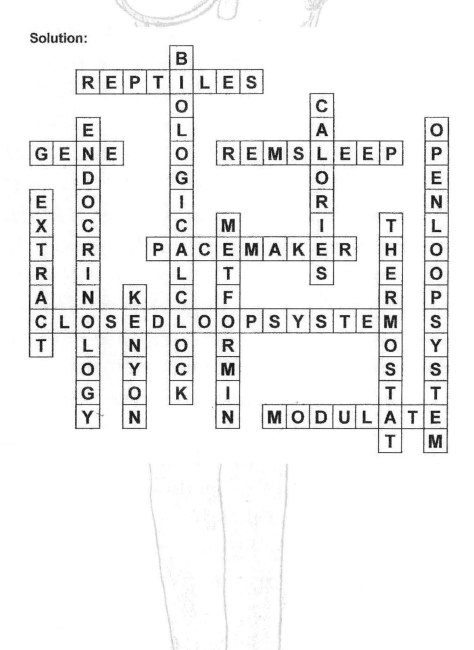

The Final Case/Circle of Life

Vocabulary 1: Definitions

Directions: Use the text, a dictionary, or the internet to write a definition for each term.

1. trends: __a general change in a situation or way people are behaving__

2. metastatic: __to spread out, as cancer often spreads from primary site to other organs__

3. chemotherapy: __treatment of illness, especially cancer, by use of cytotoxic chemicals and other drugs__

4. radiation therapy: __the treatment of disease, especially cancer, using x-rays and other forms of radiation__

5. immune system: __our body's defense against organisms and other invaders__

6. Dr. Jennifer Doudna: __a professor at UC Berkeley and a primary investigator of CRISPR__

7. CRISPR: __a genome editing tool that modifies DNA to correct undesirable traits or mutations__

8. circle of life: __the symbolic representation of birth, survival, and death, followed by new life__

9. death: __the end of life__

10. medical directive: __a document, also called a living will, that specifies what actions should be taken regarding one's health when they are no longer capable of making those decisions__

11. euthanasia: __the painless killing of a patient suffering from an incurable and painful disease__

Directions: Match the descriptions on the right to the terms on the left.

1. __F__ trends

2. __D__ metastatic

3. __H__ chemotherapy

4. __C__ radiation therapy

5. __I__ immune system

6. __K__ Dr. Jennifer Doudna

7. __B__ CRISPR

8. __G__ circle of life

9. __A__ death

10. __E__ medical directive

11. __J__ euthanasia

a. the end of life

b. a genome editing tool that modifies DNA to correct undesirable traits or mutations

c. the treatment of disease, especially cancer, using x-rays and other forms of radiation

d. to spread out, as cancer often spreads from primary site to other organs

e. a document, also called a living will, that specifies what actions should be taken regarding one's health when they are no longer capable of making those decisions

f. a general change in a situation or way people are behaving

g. the symbolic representation of birth, survival, and death, followed by new life

h. treatment of illness, especially cancer, by use of cytotoxic chemicals and other drugs

i. our body's defense against organisms and other invaders

j. the painless killing of a patient suffering from an incurable and painful disease

k. a professor at UC Berkeley and a primary investigator of CRISPR

Investigation 3.14A/B

The Final Case/Circle of Life

Vocabulary 3: Sentences

Dr. _____

P._____Date_____

Directions: Use each term in a complete sentence.

1. trends: _____

_____

2. metastatic: _____

_____

3. chemotherapy: _____

_____

4. radiation therapy: _____

_____

5. immune system: _____

_____

6. Dr. Jennifer Doudna: _____

_____

7. CRISPR: _____

_____

8. circle of life: _____

_____

9. death: _____

_____

10. medical directive: _____

_____

11. euthanasia: _____

_____

Reflections

Directions: Reflect on your reading of this investigation to answer the following questions.

1. In what way are cancer cells different from normal cells?
    Normal cells have strong attachments to similar type cells; cancer cell lack a

    bond of attachment, so they tend to spread out (metastasize).

2. Name three possible treatments for cancer:
    a. **chemotherapy**

    b. **radiation therapy**

    c. **surgery**

3. What is the negative aspect of treating cancer with chemotherapy drugs and radiation?

    Normal cells are damaged or killed along with cancer cells.

4. DNA is an acronym for: **deoxyribonucleic acid**

5. Where can DNA be found? in all living cells (but not red blood cells)

6. What is the name of the leading scientist in CRISPRS technology?

    Dr. Jennifer Doudna

7. What does the acronym CRISPR stand for?

    Clusters of Regularly Interspaced Short Palindromic Repeats

8. Name three causes of DNA mistakes or defects:
    a. **virus infection**   (any three**)**

    b. **toxic material exposure**

    c. **radiation exposure**

    d. **random mutation**

9. Briefly summarize how CRISPRS works?
   The damaged or undesirable gene is cut out from its location in the chain and replaced

   with a healthy or desirable similar gene

10. Explain how the advance in technology has both helped and harmed life on Earth.
    Genetically modified insects can reduce the spread of disease. Genetic diseases can

    potentially be edited out of the offspring DNA to eliminate heredity defects. On the

    other hand, unethical use could produce "super off-spring" or "designer babies

    matching their parents' wishes.

11. How do you feel about our potential ability to modify the DNA of children stricken with
    genetic disorders? Do you feel we should be changing the natural order? Why or why
    not?
    (student response)   sample:
    Altering damaged genetic structure to eliminate human suffering appears to be a good

    thing. History has demonstrated that good ideas misused end up displaying negative

    results. Time will tell.

12. Write a paragraph addressing your feelings about the moral obligation of scientists
    concerning potential misuses of CRISTRS technology in the future. (student response)

_____

_____

_____

_____

_____

_____

_____

_____

_____

Reflections

Directions: Answer the following based on your reading of Investigation 3.14B: Final Case.

1. Why is the "Circle of Life" inevitable for every living thing?

   Death is inevitable at some point for all living things.

2. What does it mean for a patient to be 'terminal'?

   A terminal patient is thought to be in their last days, weeks, or months of life.

3. What is one of the most difficult duties physicians have?

   Among the most difficult duties a physician has involved telling loved ones or patients that there is no longer hope for treatment or cure of their illness, especially if the patient is a child or young adult. Most people have great difficulty dealing with the subject of death.

4. Do all patients and their families agree on end of life decisions? Explain

   Many patients and their families do NOT agree on end of life decisions, many because they do not address the issue BEFORE a death is imminent.

5. What is a 'medical directive'?

   A medical directive is a legal document instructing about the wishes of the individual whose life is potentially about to end how they would like to be treated at the time they are no longer personally able to make decisions for themselves.

6. Since we never know which day will be our last day living on this Earth, what can we do to enhance our lives and those of our friends and family? (sample response)

   Since we truly never know when our last living day will occur, it is wise to live each day as though it was your last, treating others with respect and doing positive things for humanity while you can.

Directions: Use the highlighted terms in the chapter to solve the puzzle. Most clues come from the chapter text, some require outside investigation. Omit spaces or dashes between words.

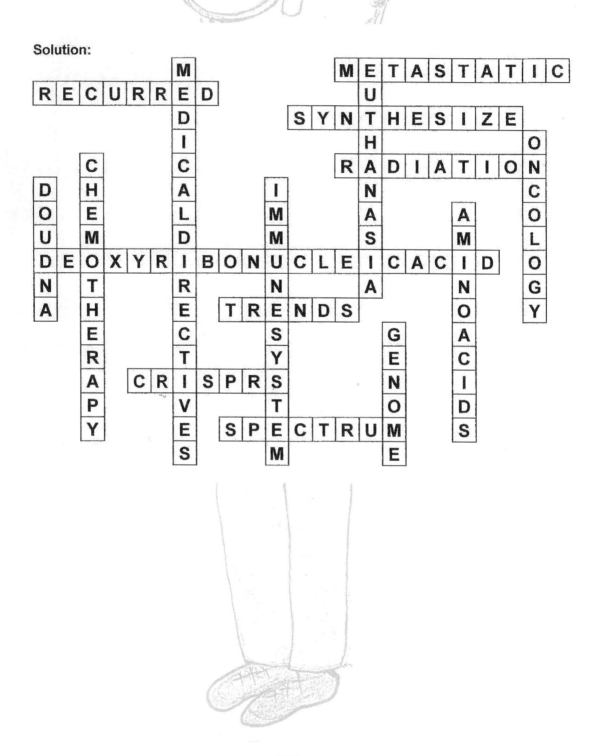

Solution:

					M										M	E	T	A	S	T	A	T	I	C

R E C U R R E D

MEDICALDLD column

M E T A S T A T I C

S Y N T H E S I Z E

R A D I A T I O N

O N C O L O G Y

C H E M O T H E R A P Y

D O U D E N A

D E O X Y R I B O N U C L E I C A C I D

T R E N D S

C R I S P R S

S P E C T R U M

G E N O M E

A M I N O A C I D S

I M M U N E S Y S T E M

Looking Deeper

Vocabulary 1: Definitions

Directions: Use the text, a dictionary, or the internet to write a definition for each term.

1. history & physical: _ **the part of medical practice based on experience and intuition**

    _____

2. differential diagnosis:_ **a method to explore more fully the causes and effects of a**

    particular problem _____

3. experience: ____ **refers to the number of times one has performed an activity** ____

    _____

4. art of medical practice: _ **familiarity with a skill or field of knowledge acquired over**

    month or years, presumably resulting in additional expertise in that field _____

5. science of medical practice: _ **the part of medical practice based on actual scientific**

    knowledge _____

6. 5-whys: _ **a method to explore more fully the causes and effects of a particular** _____

    problem _____

7. Write an example of deeper thinking using the "5-Whys": (student's thoughts)

    a. _____

       _____

    b. _____

       _____

    c. _____

       _____

    d. _____

       _____

    e. _____

       _____

Investigation 3.15

Looking Deeper

Vocabulary 2: Matching

Directions: Match the descriptions on the right to the terms on the left.

1. __C__ history & physical

2. __E__ differential diagnosis

3. __A__ experience

4. __D__ art of medical practice

5. __B__ science of medical practice

6. __F__ 5-whys

a. familiarity with a skill or field of knowledge acquired over month or years, presumably resulting in additional expertise in that field

b. the part of medical practice based on actual scientific knowledge

c. the part of the patient visit where the physician learns about the changes in the patient's health and the observations that help make the diagnosis

d. the part of medical practice based on experience and intuition

e. the list of possible causes of the symptoms and objective findings

f. a method to explore more fully the causes and effects of a particular problem

Investigation 3.15

Looking Deeper

Vocabulary 3: Sentences

Name: _____

Period_____Date_____

Directions: Use each term in a complete sentence. Then write another example using 5-whys.

1. history & physical: _____

     _____

2. differential diagnosis:_____

     _____

3. experience: _____

     _____

4. art of medical practice: _____

     _____

5. science of medical practice: _____

     _____

6. 5-whys: _____

     _____

7. Write another example of deeper thinking using the "5-Whys":

     a. _____

          _____

     b. _____

          _____

     c. _____

          _____

     d. _____

          _____

     e. _____

          _____

Investigation 3.15   Teacher

Crossword 3.15   **Looking Deeper/ 5 Whys**

Directions: Use the highlighted terms in the chapter to solve the puzzle. Most clues come from the chapter text, some require outside investigation. Omit spaces or dashes between words.

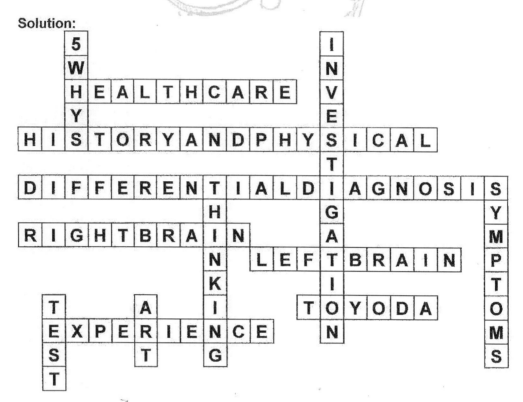

Solution:

```
        5
        W                           I
        H E A L T H C A R E         N
        Y                           V
H I S T O R Y A N D P H Y S         I C A L
        D I F F E R E N T I A L D I A G N O S I S
                      H           I G               Y
R I G H T B R A I N   N           A                 M
                      N   L E F T B R A I N          P
                      K           I                  T
    T           A     I         T O Y O D A          O
    E X P E R I E N C E           N                  M
    S           T     G                              S
    T
```

260

Congratulations! You have successfully completed a journey into the world of the medical practitioner. If you completed all of the assignments, you earned the Certificate of Completion of Medical Investigation 101 on the final page. You may carefully remove the certificate from the workbook, add your name, frame, and hang proudly on your wall. You now have a better understanding of the thought process required to solve the medical investigations so important and meaningful to your patients' well-being. This same process of asking "why" and looking deeper can work in your daily life as a student and well beyond as you strive to make good life decisions.

You also appreciate now that, regardless of your future occupation, solving significant problems of all types often requires collaboration and teamwork. Complex issues benefit from the input of people with a diversity of training, experience, and insight. In almost any career you will work with others to find the successful solutions to the challenges you face. Individuals you trust can prove essential for even personal problems you may face in the years ahead. Many successful people actually create their own personal "Board of Directors" to call on for advice when they make important decisions. We wish you a successful journey as you solve the challenges and investigations in your life. No life completely avoids stress and difficulty, but we hope some of the lessons you have learned in this introduction to medical investigation make you better able to make sound decisions. Thanks for allowing us into your life.

In his youth **Dr. Russ Hill** imagined himself playing professional baseball, encouraged by a successful high school baseball career. But higher levels of competition failed to ratify that expectation, so he had to pursue his backup plan. In college he trained for teaching, but upon graduation no jobs were open. Instead he found an opportunity in pharmaceutical sales. While doing that work he met a Podiatrist who was an alumnus of Dr. Hill's own high school. The doctor challenged him to further his science education and then apply to Podiatry school. He did and at the end of a career in health care he retired, still feeling the need for challenges in his life.

In pursuit of another challenge, Dr. Hill followed his daughter into the teaching profession, a profession he originally had pursued over twenty years earlier. Over the past decade and a half he has challenged his students to bump up their own aspirations, just as the Podiatrist had done for him. He still teaches middle school Science and STEM.

The current trend in education has put a focus on career readiness, and yet we have not seen a textbook that introduces students to medically-oriented careers. This one tries to do just that by providing insights into how doctors analyze problems and conduct medical investigations. Whether students end up with a medically oriented career or not, the analytical skills required of physicians have applications in almost all careers we expect to see opening up in the future. Besides, It never hurts to have some basic medical knowledge tucked away when collaborating with a physician to maintain your own good health.

Dr. Richard Griffith never imagined a career in medicine when he was your age. Instead electronics fascinated him at a time when America was very excited about going into outer space. He took math and physics in a small town high school from a former mining engineer who encouraged him to ask why, and challenge the simple answers to questions. In college he studied physics, but eventually recognized that his passion lay in solving everyday problems and not so much finding new sub-atomic particles. He went to graduate school in electrical engineering and got interested in medical applications for engineering tools. He got career guidance from an older engineer who had attended medical school and eventually became a researcher at the National Institutes of Health. Based on his advice, Griffith completed a doctorate in electrical engineering and then applied to medical school, frankly not expecting to get accepted since biology and chemistry were not a significant part of his prior studies. To his surprise they let him in and he managed to transition into this very different mode of thinking and learning.

His electrical engineering background got him involved in research in neurosurgery even before he finished medical school, but he decided that he needed a clinical specialty for a successful career, so he selected a residency in anesthesiology. That specialty seemed to best suit his array of interests. He since has done private practice, worked as a medical director in a major medical device company, and finally finished his career in academic medicine teaching medical students and resident physicians. Now retired in Vermont, he has been working to involve industrial designers more fully in the cause of Patient Safety, because mistakes in health care have become an alarmingly common occurrence despite the best intentions of health care professionals. It appears that industrial designers have some unique skills that may prove especially valuable in the future of safer medical care.

Russ Hill and Richard Griffith are First Cousins who grew up on opposite sides of this country, Griffith in Virginia and Hill in California. Griffith's Mother was the Sister of Hill's Father. Griffith was thirteen and Hill was eleven when they first met. Griffith's family had driven west for his Father to attend a summer workshop in economics and to visit their distant Hill relatives. They made that 6,000 miles round trip in the middle of summer with no radio or air conditioner in their car. Times were tough back then. The two cousins did not see one other in person again until seventeen years later when Hill's family visited the Griffith family in Virginia. In the ensuing years they have communicated by email as their friendship grew. They have gotten together a few times in New York, Montana, and Vermont, where Griffith now lives. In spite of the geographical barrier, they successfully collaborated by many e-mails for over a year in order to write this book.

Raella Hill married Russ more than 45 years ago, first meeting him in high school. She worked in hospitals before taking several years off to raise her two children. She then studied art and immersed herself in ceramics, photography, painting, and printmaking. Her final career job was as office manager for architectural photographers. Her interests now include her four grandchildren, printmaking, and yoga.

May all who gaze upon
this Certificate know--

has diligently and steadfastly
completed all the work
required to be known
now and for all time as
an official, certified
MEDICAL SCIENCE
INVESTIGATION 101
trained practitioner.

This official diploma and its conferred title is awarded by Dr's. Hill and Griffith
without any authority given them by any organization or government, but is nonetheless
well deserved by every student who has read Medical Science Investigation 101 and
done all the assigned tasks in the accompanying workbook. Congratulations to you.
Keep exercising your mind and working toward making this a better and safer world.

Made in the USA
Middletown, DE
26 August 2022